I'm Dreaming of a chocolate christmas

other books by marcel desaulniers

The Trellis Cookbook

Death by Chocolate

The Burger Meisters

Desserts to Die For

An Alphabet of Sweets

Death by Chocolate Cookies

Salad Days

Death by Chocolate Cakes

Celebrate with Chocolate

I'm Dreaming of a chocolate christmas

marcel desaulniers

Author of *Death by Chocolate*

PHOTOGRAPHY BY RON MANVILLE

John Wiley & Sons, Inc.

This book is printed on acid-free paper. ♾

Published by John Wiley & Sons, Inc., Hoboken, New Jersey

Published simultaneously in Canada

For general information on our other products and services or for technical support, please contact our Customer Care Department within the United States at (800) 762-2974, outside the United States at (317) 572-3993 or fax (317) 572-4002.

Wiley publishes in a variety of print and electronic formats and by print-on-demand. Some material included with standard print versions of this book may not be included in e-books or in print-on-demand. If this book refers to media such as a CD or DVD that is not included in the version you purchased, you may download this material at http://booksupport.wiley.com. For more information about Wiley products, visit www.wiley.com.

Interior design by Joel Avirom and Jason Snyder

Library of Congress Cataloging-in-Publication Data:

Desaulniers, Marcel.

I'm dreaming of a chocolate Christmas / Marcel Desaulniers; photography by Ron Manville.

p. cm.

Includes bibliographical references and index.

ISBN: 978-1-118-38356-8 (pbk), ISBN: 978-1-118-06038-4 (ebk), ISBN: 978-1-118-06039-1 (ebk), ISBN: 978-1-118-06041-4 (ebk)

1. Cookery (Chocolate) 2. Chocolate desserts. 3. Christmas cookery. I. Title.

TX767.C5D475 2007

641.6'374--dc22

2006036929

Printed in the United States of America

10 9 8 7 6 5 4 3 2

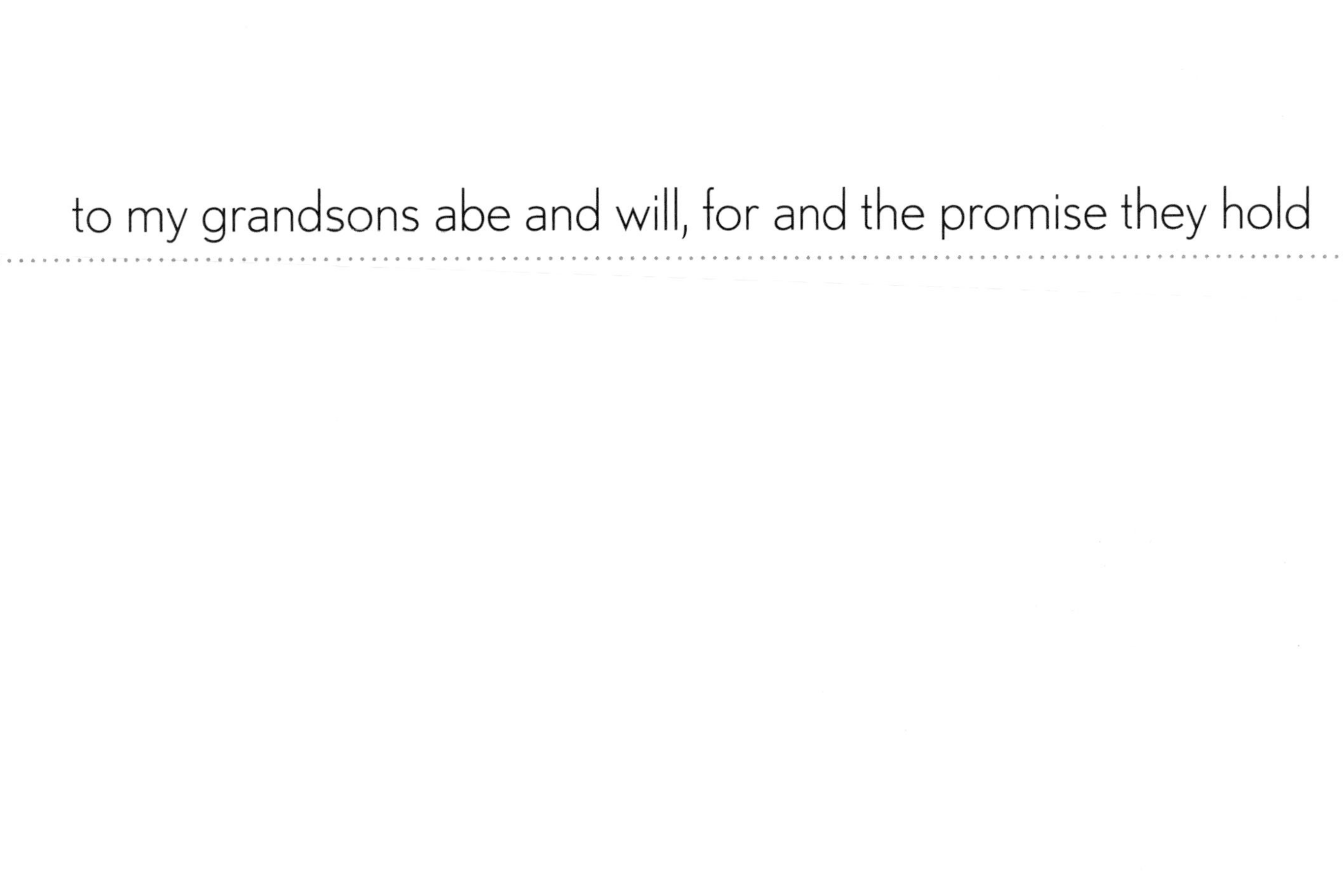

to my grandsons abe and will, for and the promise they hold

contents

acknowledgments

My wife Connie, you are the light and love of my life

Dan Green, literary agent

Justin Schwartz, editor

Shelley Tennant, recipe assistant

Ron Manville, photographer, a true professional

John Curtis, business partner

Penny Seu, editorial advisor

Michael Holdsworth, The Trellis chef

Sarah Masters, The Trellis senior assistant chef

Michelle Holdsworth, The Trellis assistant chef

Christina Moulliet, The Trellis assistant chef

Heather Lenhardt, The Trellis pastry chef

Bridget Young, The Culinary Institute of America pastry extern

The Trellis kitchen, management, front-of-the-house, and office staff

Christine Manville, prop assistant

Nancy Thomas, prop contributor

Irina Zaytceva, prop contributor

The students, instructors, and staff at The Culinary Institute of America

introduction

oh! you better watch out,

or you'll find yourself as frantic as one of Santa's elves on December 23, baking complicated desserts for friends and family for the holiday. Instead, you can use the recipes in this book—they are simple and straightforward, but still loaded with "WOW!" Honestly. As the author of *Death by Chocolate* (the seven-layer namesake dessert is three pages long and takes three days to make), I'm not knocking elaborate desserts. I'm just saying: Use my other baking books the rest of the year and this one during the holidays, because parties are going on.

you better not cry

as your fudge crystallizes in its scorched pan, or your favorite Christmas cake turns into an avalanche. The recipes in *I'm Dreaming of a Chocolate Christmas* are simple *and* fail-safe. We tested them in a home kitchen using equipment and ingredients found in local stores. Most were tested three to five times—or more. My wife Connie, who can't cook at all, could read and understand the recipes. We experimented with numerous ways to store, cool, reheat, and eat. We simplified steps to make less room for error and more room for flavor. If you find that a recipe in this book doesn't work to your satisfaction, please e-mail me at goganache@aol.com, and I'll help you through it.

better not pout

while your friends are going to Christmas parties, and you're cleaning pots and baking pans. I certainly can't help you wash pans, but I will tell you that some of the recipes in this book use only one bowl, one spoon, and one pan to make. Many don't use an electric mixer, and you can simplify making plenty of the recipes by preparing the easy steps over several days. *I'm Dreaming of a Chocolate Christmas* has only one complex dessert—the Pumpkin Pecan Caramel Chocolate Fudge Ice Cream Cake (see Baby, It's Cold Outside, page 60)—but it's worth the trouble, and it is really five simple desserts rolled into one. Please note: Many of the recipes would be so much fun to bake with kids that you'll forget about the parties—and the kids can wash a pan or two in exchange for your sweet reward.

i'm telling you why:

You want to have your cake and Christmas, too. You want to share your creations with your friends, without it costing an arm and a leg and a week in the kitchen. You want to ship, store, give, take, reheat, and eat these desserts, knowing they will be delicious. And you want to have time to enjoy the holidays without hindering your love of baking. After all, ***Santa Claus is coming.***

home for the holidays

chocolate fruitycakes

MAKES 12 MINI CAKES

See photo, page xiv

If you use fruitcake as a doorstop, then make room in your house (and heart) for a truly appealing chocolate version, bejeweled with fruit, studded with walnuts, spiked with vivacious spices, and splashed with whiskey. Katie, bar the door—the spirit of the holidays has been redefined!

8 tablespoons (1 stick) unsalted butter, cut into 1-tablespoon pieces, plus 2 tablespoons, melted

1½ cups plus 2 tablespoons all-purpose flour

½ cup unsweetened cocoa powder

½ teaspoon baking powder

¼ teaspoon baking soda

¼ teaspoon salt

⅛ teaspoon ground cinnamon

⅛ teaspoon ground cloves

⅛ teaspoon ground mace

1 cup walnut halves, toasted (see Techniques, page 192) and chopped by hand into ¼-inch pieces

½ cup dried cherries

½ cup raisins

¼ cup ¼-inch pieces candied lemon rind

¼ cup ¼-inch pieces candied orange rind

¼ cup ¼-inch pieces dried pineapple

½ cup ¼-inch pieces pitted prunes

¾ cup granulated sugar

3 large eggs

12 ounces semisweet baking chocolate, coarsely chopped and melted (see Techniques, page 191)

1 cup sour cream

¼ cup pure Grade A dark amber maple syrup

¾ cup whiskey

GARNISH

Cranberry Marmalade or Cranberry "Punch" Sorbet (see Santa's Workshop, pages 167 and 168)

1. Preheat the oven to 325°F.

2. Refrigerate 2 sets of nonstick, fluted mini tube pans, each with 6 individual inserts, for 5 minutes. Remove the pans from the refrigerator. Using a pastry brush, thoroughly coat the inside of each insert with the 2 tablespoons melted butter, being sure that all of the indentations are completely coated. Refrigerate until needed. (The pans need to be refrigerated to allow the butter to adhere to the nonstick surface.)

3. In a sifter, combine 1½ cups of the flour, the cocoa, baking powder, baking soda, salt, cinnamon, cloves, and mace. Sift onto a large piece of parchment or wax paper.

4. Place the walnuts, cherries, raisins, lemon and orange rind, pineapple, and prunes in a medium bowl. Sprinkle the remaining 2 tablespoons flour over the nuts and fruits, and gently toss to coat lightly.

5. Place the sugar and the remaining 8 tablespoons butter in the bowl of a stand electric mixer fitted with a paddle. Mix on low for 1 minute, then beat on medium for 2 minutes, until soft. Stop and scrape down the sides of the bowl and the paddle.

Beat on medium for an additional 2 minutes, until very soft. Scrape down again. Add the eggs one at a time, beating on medium for 30 seconds after each addition, and scraping down again once all the eggs have been incorporated. (Don't be concerned that the batter looks curdled; it will come together by the time the whiskey is added.) Add the melted chocolate and mix on medium for 15 to 20 seconds, until incorporated. Scrape down again.

6. Turn the mixer on low and gradually add the dry ingredients; mix until incorporated, about 15 seconds. Scrape down again. Add the sour cream and beat on medium for 10 to 15 seconds to incorporate. With the mixer on the lowest speed, add the maple syrup and ½ cup of the whiskey, mixing until combined, about 30 seconds (notice the batter is smooth now that the whiskey has been added). Remove the bowl from the mixer and scrape down again. Add the flour-coated walnuts and dried fruit, using a rubber spatula to mix until thoroughly combined.

7. Portion 5 heaping tablespoons or 1 heaping #12 ice-cream scoop into each tube pan. Place the pans on the center rack of the oven and bake until a toothpick inserted in the center of the cakes comes out clean, about 28 minutes, rotating each set of pans 180 degrees halfway through the baking time.

8. Remove from the oven and cool for 5 minutes. Invert the pans to release the cakes onto a cooling rack (the longer the cakes stay in the pans, the more difficult it will be to release them).

9. Use a pastry brush to moisten the top and sides of the cakes with the remaining ¼ cup whiskey. (For a more pronounced whiskey flavor, brush the cakes with the same amount of whiskey the next day.) Once the cakes have cooled to room temperature, place them in a tightly sealed plastic container and store at room temperature.

PRESENTATION Although the Fruitycakes are perfect for shipping, they also make for a bountiful presentation when stacked high on a decorative platter for your Christmas day buffet. Complete the presentation with an accompanying bowl of Cranberry Marmalade or even the Cranberry "Punch" Sorbet. Ho, Ho, Ho!

THE CHEF'S TOUCH

Look for nonstick fluted mini tube pans in kitchenware, hardware, and department stores. The Baker's Secret® pans we purchased from our local Target store are manufactured by EKCO® Housewares Company. Each pan has six 3½ × 1¾-inch inserts.

The cakes are wonderful to eat at room temperature; however, serving them slightly warm is a transcendent experience. The cakes may be warmed in a microwave. It takes about 10 seconds on Defrost in our microwave at Ganache Hill. It may take you a few seconds more or less in your microwave, depending upon the wattage and power settings.

If you plan to produce lots of Fruitycakes for holiday gift giving, you may want to start baking before the goblins migrate in October. The cakes will keep for an extended period of time when stored in tightly sealed plastic containers. Occasionally brush the cakes very lightly with additional whiskey to ensure that they will be at their prime in late December.

For shipping, I recommend that you plastic wrap each Fruitycake, then place them in a plastic container with crumpled tissue paper protecting the cakes. Seal the container, and you are ready to pack for shipping.

karen's chocolate peppermint bourbon walnut fudge

MAKES ABOUT 3 POUNDS

O fudge—how we love you for tempting us as you do in this recipe, with a dark and dense mélange of chocolate, walnuts, bourbon, and peppermint. Fudge, you are not just candy. You are olfactory and gustatory ecstasy, and we shall eat every last morsel before the gentleman and his reindeer hit the scene.

4 tablespoons (½ stick) unsalted butter, cut into 1-tablespoon pieces, plus 1 tablespoon, melted

3⅓ cups granulated sugar

1⅓ cups heavy cream

1 teaspoon salt

16 ounces semisweet baking chocolate, coarsely chopped

1 cup walnut halves, toasted (see Techniques, page 192) and coarsely chopped

1 tablespoon bourbon

1 tablespoon peppermint extract

1. Lightly coat an 8 × 8 × 2–inch nonstick baking pan with the 1 tablespoon melted butter, then line the pan with plastic wrap.

2. Combine the sugar, cream, the remaining 4 tablespoons butter, and the salt in a medium saucepan over medium heat. Bring to a boil, stirring frequently to completely dissolve the sugar. Turn the heat down (so the mixture does not boil out of the saucepan), and continue to boil while stirring frequently until the mixture reaches a temperature of 230°F (thread stage), about 6 minutes. Use a digital thermometer (see Equipment, page 186) for an accurate reading.

3. Remove from the heat. Add the chopped chocolate and stir carefully with a whisk. Stir until the chocolate has melted and been completely incorporated. Add the walnuts, bourbon, and peppermint extract, and stir with a rubber spatula until incorporated. Pour the fudge into the prepared pan, spreading evenly with the spatula. Cover with plastic wrap and refrigerate until firm, about 2 hours.

4. To serve, remove the top layer of plastic wrap. Flip the pan upside down on top of a cutting board. Remove the plastic wrap. Cut into desired size pieces. Store in tightly sealed plastic container in the refrigerator. Bring to room temperature before serving.

THE CHEF'S TOUCH

This book did not originally include a fudge recipe because my mom's fudge was in my first chocolate book, *Death by Chocolate*. Why go beyond Mom? Former Trellis pastry chef Shelley Tennant boldly answered that question when she presented me with a batch of her stepmother Karen's fudge. After the first bite, I knew this book needed her version. Karen, a very enthusiastic cook who was enamored with a fudge purchased in Baltimore Harbor, replicated it with this relatively foolproof and easy-to-prepare recipe.

Karen's fudge will retain all of its pepperminty delightfulness for several days stored in a tightly sealed plastic container in the refrigerator. For long-term storage (up to several weeks), freeze the fudge in a tightly sealed plastic container to prevent dehydration and to protect it from refrigerator or freezer odors. Refrigerated or frozen, the fudge will get very hard; bring it to room temperature before enjoying.

jan's oatmeal chocolate chip cake

SERVES 12

Florid prose would be appropriate for this simple-to-prepare gâteau. A harmonious union of chocolate and oatmeal, it takes one bowl, one pan, and about 15 minutes to prepare, leaving you time to wrap presents while it bakes and cools. It's all anyone could want for holiday dessert enjoyment.

8 tablespoons (1 stick) plus ½ tablespoon unsalted butter, melted

1¾ cups plus 1 tablespoon all-purpose flour

1 tablespoon unsweetened cocoa powder

1 teaspoon baking soda

½ teaspoon salt

1 cup quick oats

1¾ cups boiling water

1 cup granulated sugar

1 cup tightly packed light brown sugar

3 large eggs, whisked together

1½ cups semisweet chocolate chips

¾ cup walnut halves, toasted (see Techniques, page 192) and coarsely chopped

GARNISH

Vivacious Vanilla Ice Cream (see Santa's Workshop, page 181)

1. Preheat the oven to 350°F.

2. Lightly coat a 13 × 9 × 2–inch nonstick baking pan with 1½ tablespoon of the melted butter. Dust the pan with the tablespoon of flour and shake out any excess.

3. In a sifter, combine the remaining 1¾ cups flour, the cocoa, baking soda, and salt. Sift onto a large piece of parchment or wax paper.

4. Place the oats in a large heatproof bowl. Pour the boiling water over the oats and let stand for 10 minutes before adding the sugars, eggs, and remaining 8 tablespoons melted butter. Stir with a rubber spatula until combined. Add the dry ingredients, and use a rubber spatula to fold the ingredients until combined. Fold in 1 cup of the chocolate chips. Pour the batter into the prepared pan.

5. Combine the remaining ½ cup chocolate chips and the walnuts in a small bowl. Evenly sprinkle the chocolate chips and walnuts over the top of the batter.

6. Bake on the center rack of the oven until a toothpick inserted in the center of the cake comes out clean, about 40 minutes, rotating the pan 180 degrees halfway through the baking time.

7. Remove the cake from the oven and cool in the pan for 20 minutes at room temperature. Gently turn the cake out onto a cutting board, then turn the cake chocolate chip–nut topping side up (this is easier if you use a utility turner or wide spatula). Cool for an additional 10 minutes before cutting.

continued

PRESENTATION Heat the blade of a serrated knife under hot running water and wipe dry before cutting each portion. Serve with a scoop or two of Vivacious Vanilla Ice Cream on top.

THE CHEF'S TOUCH

Handed-down family recipes are precious for lots of folks. Jan's Oatmeal Chocolate Chip Cake, a recipe that former Trellis pastry chef Shelley Tennant was given by her late mother-in-law, Jan, is a culinary heirloom. A caring person always ready to help someone in need, Jan made this cake for her family (omitting the nuts based on family preference) and for town events such as fire-hall dinners (including the nuts for universal appeal). Nuts or not, it is a moist but sturdy cake and will withstand the rigors of the holidays.

Once it has cooled, you can store the cake in a tightly sealed plastic container at room temperature for several days. It keeps well in the refrigerator, similarly contained, for up to 10 days. By the way, Jan's Oatmeal Chocolate Chip Cake is an excellent candidate for shipping (see Dessert Giving, page 195).

chocolate cherry muffins

MAKES 24 MUFFINS

How evocative of the holidays is the sweet smell of muffins baking in the oven! But instead of the ubiquitous bran and raisin variety, this Christmastime muffin embraces chocolate, chocolate chips, and cherries. It's beginning to smell a lot like Christmas . . .

2½ cups plus 1 tablespoon all-purpose flour

½ cup unsweetened cocoa powder

½ cup granulated sugar

1½ teaspoons baking powder

¾ teaspoon baking soda

½ teaspoon salt

2 cups dried tart red cherries

¾ cup vegetable oil

4 ounces semisweet baking chocolate, coarsely chopped

1 cup buttermilk

2 large eggs

½ cup tightly packed light brown sugar

¼ cup honey

1 cup semisweet chocolate chips

½ cup walnut halves, toasted (see Techniques, page 192) and coarsely chopped

1. Preheat the oven to 350°F. Line each of the 24 muffin tin cups with 2½-inch foil or paper liners.

2. In a sifter, combine 2½ cups of the flour, the cocoa, granulated sugar, baking powder, baking soda, and salt. Sift onto a large piece of parchment or wax paper.

3. Place the cherries in a small bowl and dust them with the remaining tablespoon of flour.

4. Heat the oil and the chopped chocolate in the top of a double boiler or in a medium glass bowl in a microwave oven (see Techniques, page 191), and stir until melted and smooth.

5. Place the buttermilk, melted chocolate, eggs, brown sugar, and honey in a large mixing bowl. Use a whisk to mix until the ingredients are thoroughly combined and the brown sugar has almost completely dissolved. Add the dry ingredients, and stir with a rubber spatula to combine. Add the cherries, chocolate chips, and walnuts, using the spatula to fold the ingredients together thoroughly.

6. Portion 3 slightly heaping tablespoons or 1 slightly heaping #20 ice-cream scoop of batter into each muffin cup. Place the muffin tins on the top and center racks of the oven, and bake until a toothpick inserted in the center of the muffins comes out almost clean, about 16 minutes if you prefer slightly underbaked (yum), and 18 minutes for fully baked. (Switch the tins between top and center and rotate each 180 degrees halfway through the baking time.)

continued

7. Remove the muffin tins from the oven, and cool at room temperature for 15 minutes. Remove the muffins from the muffin tins (but not from the liners), and cool at room temperature for an additional 20 minutes. I enjoy these muffins slightly warm or at room temperature.

THE CHEF'S TOUCH

Packed with fifteen different ingredients, most found in the typical home pantry, these muffins deliver no shortage of mouth-warming, chocolaty flavor, every bite punctuated by the snap of tart red cherries. Just the type of mini cake to have on hand for visiting friends and family.

Once cooled, the muffins may be stored in a tightly sealed plastic container at room temperature for several days. They may also be frozen, similarly contained to avoid picking up odors, for up to 3 weeks. Bring to room temperature before serving.

mike's dark chocolate black bottom bites

MAKES 24 BITES

Black bottom pie has many confectionery cousins, including Mike's Black Bottom Bites, a delicate little bite of not-too-sweet cocoa cake spiked with rum and packed with a cream cheese filling. Please, oh, please, Santa, bring me some Bites.

BLACK BOTTOM BITES BATTER

1 tablespoon unsalted butter, melted

1 cup plus 2 tablespoons all-purpose flour

¾ cup granulated sugar

⅓ cup unsweetened cocoa powder

¼ teaspoon salt

¾ cup warm water (about 100°F)

⅓ cup vegetable oil

2 teaspoons dark rum (preferably Myers's®)

1½ cups semisweet chocolate mini morsels

CREAM CHEESE FILLING

One 8-ounce package cream cheese, softened

3 tablespoons granulated sugar

Pinch of salt

1 large egg yolk

MAKE THE BLACK BOTTOM BITES BATTER:

1. Preheat the oven to 350°F. Coat 24 nonstick mini muffin cups with the melted butter.

2. In a sifter, combine the flour, sugar, cocoa, and salt. Sift into a large bowl. Add the water, oil, and rum and stir with a whisk until thoroughly combined (the batter will be lumpy—not to worry). Add the chocolate morsels, and use a rubber spatula to fold them into the batter.

MAKE THE CREAM CHEESE FILLING:

3. Place the cream cheese, sugar, and salt in the bowl of a stand electric mixer fitted with a paddle. Mix on low for 1 minute, then beat on medium-high for 2 minutes. Stop and scrape down the sides of the bowl and the paddle. Add the egg yolk and beat on medium for 30 seconds, until combined. Remove the bowl from the mixer, and use a rubber spatula to finish mixing the filling until thoroughly combined.

continued

4. Portion slightly less than 1 level tablespoon or slightly less than 1 level #70 ice-cream scoop of batter into each muffin cup. Now spoon 1 heaping teaspoon of the cream cheese filling on top of the batter, and finally top off with slightly less than 1 level tablespoon or scoop of batter. Place the muffin tins on the center rack of the oven and bake until a toothpick inserted in the center of a Bite comes out clean, about 12 minutes (rotate the tins 180 degrees halfway through the baking time). Remove from the oven, and cool the Bites at room temperature in the muffin cups for 10 minutes. Invert the cups to release the Bites onto a cooling rack, and allow to cool for another 15 minutes. The cooled Bites may be stored in a tightly sealed container for up to 1 week.

THE CHEF'S TOUCH

The memory of a shared recipe is often personal and comforting. I spent many hours with my mom in her kitchen in Woonsocket, Rhode Island, watching her bake as she shared her knowledge. Former Trellis pastry chef Shelley Tennant has similar cherished memories. Although her dad, Mike, admitted he was not a great baker, he had one recipe that was exceptional and eagerly anticipated by his family. That would be his Black Bottom Bites. Shelley remembers the specific Christmas that her dad passed his recipe along to her, when at only twelve, she had already developed a keen interest in baking.

Many recipes for black bottom pie and its derivatives abound; however, only Mike's Black Bottom Bites have been proclaimed by Santa as "best in the land."

chocolate chip pecan rum tart

SERVES 8

A slim tart with a mighty big chocolate flavor, the Chocolate Chip Pecan Rum Tart begins with a sugar cookie crust as a delicious platform for a dense caramel filling studded with chocolate chips and pecans and suffused with rum. Remember that big things come in small packages, both under the tree and with this tart.

SWEET AND SOUR SUGAR COOKIE CRUST

Sweet and Sour Sugar Cookies (see Santa's Workshop, page 169), unbaked

¼ cup all-purpose flour

1 tablespoon unsalted butter, melted

CHOCOLATE CHIP PECAN RUM TART FILLING

1 cup pecan halves, toasted (see Techniques, page 192) and finely chopped

½ cup semisweet chocolate chips

1 large egg plus 1 large egg yolk

⅓ cup tightly packed light brown sugar

2 tablespoons heavy cream

2 tablespoons molasses

2 tablespoons dark rum

⅛ teaspoon salt

2½ tablespoons unsalted butter, melted

GARNISH

Vivacious Vanilla Ice Cream (see Santa's Workshop, page 181)

MAKE THE CRUST:

1. Preheat the oven to 325°F. Weigh out 10 ounces of the dough and transfer to a clean, dry, lightly floured work surface and knead gently to form a smooth ball. (The remaining dough can be frozen or baked into cookies.) Wrap in plastic wrap and refrigerate for 20 minutes. Coat a 9 × 1–inch tart pan with the melted butter.

2. Remove the dough from the refrigerator and remove the plastic wrap. Place the dough on a clean, dry, lightly floured work surface. Dust a rolling pin with flour and roll the dough into a circle 10 inches in diameter and ⅛ inch thick. Line the prepared tart pan with the dough, gently pressing it into the bottom and sides of the pan. Use your hands to trim any excess dough flush with the sides of the pan. Use a fork to prick the crust in several places. Line the bottom of the crust with aluminum foil, and bake on the center rack of the oven for 15 minutes. Remove the foil and bake for an additional 10 minutes, until very light golden brown. Remove from the oven and set aside while making the filling. Leave the oven turned on to 325°F.

MAKE THE CHOCOLATE CHIP PECAN RUM TART FILLING:

3. Place the pecans, chocolate chips, egg, egg yolk, sugar, cream, molasses, rum, and salt in a large bowl. Use a whisk to combine the ingredients. Add the melted butter and stir to incorporate. Pour the mixture into the crust and bake on the center rack of the oven until the filling is slightly firm to the touch, about 25 minutes. (Halfway through the baking time, rotate the tart 180 degrees.)

continued

4. Remove the tart from the oven and cool at room temperature on a cooling rack for 10 minutes, then refrigerate the tart for 1 hour before serving. Remove the tart from the pan. Heat the blade of a serrated knife under hot running water, and wipe dry before making each slice. The tart may be served directly from the refrigerator or allowed to stay at room temperature for 15 minutes or so (I prefer it that way). Serve with a scoop or two of Vivacious Vanilla Ice Cream.

THE CHEF'S TOUCH

This tart is pecan pie on steroids, with a jolt of chocolate and the zing of rum. (No wonder it was actually Santa, not Blackbeard, who said, "Ho, Ho, Ho and a bottle of . . . ") I love the ease of preparing the filling, but most of all I love eating it!

If you want to spread out the preparation, make the dough and line the tart pan as directed, then freeze it for several days or even for a couple of weeks. Wrap the pan tightly with plastic wrap to prevent freezer burn. Bring the cookie dough–lined tart pan to room temperature before baking.

After assembly, you may keep the Chocolate Chip Pecan Rum Tart in the refrigerator up to 3 days before serving. To prevent the tart from absorbing refrigerator odors, store it in a tightly sealed plastic container.

they're nutty chocolate brownies

MAKES 12 TO 24 BROWNIES

Is it all in the name? A brownie is, after all, a type of cake. So why does a "brownie" seem so much more . . . fun? The answer is easy when it's "They're Nutty Chocolate Brownies." Dense, moist, chocolaty, fudgy, chock-full of nuts, and lavishly topped with ganache—now that's a BROWNIE!

THEY'RE NUTTY CHOCOLATE BROWNIES

12 tablespoons (1½ sticks) unsalted butter, cut into 1-tablespoon pieces, plus 1 tablespoon, melted

1 cup plus 2 tablespoons all-purpose flour

6 ounces unsweetened baking chocolate, coarsely chopped

1 teaspoon salt

½ teaspoon baking powder

5 large eggs

1 cup granulated sugar

½ cup buttermilk

3 tablespoons dark corn syrup

1 tablespoon pure vanilla extract

1½ cups pecan halves, toasted (see Techniques, page 192) and coarsely chopped

1½ cups walnut halves, toasted and coarsely chopped

DARK CHOCOLATE GANACHE

4 ounces unsweetened baking chocolate, coarsely chopped

2 ounces semisweet baking chocolate, coarsely chopped

1 cup heavy cream

MAKE THE THEY'RE NUTTY CHOCOLATE BROWNIES:

1. Preheat the oven to 325°F. Lightly coat an 8 × 8 × 2–inch nonstick baking pan with the 1 tablespoon melted butter. Sprinkle the pan with 2 tablespoons flour; shake out any excess.

2. Melt the chocolate and the remaining 12 tablespoons butter in a double boiler or in a small glass bowl in a microwave oven (see Techniques, page 191) and stir until smooth.

3. In a sifter, combine the remaining 1 cup flour, the salt, and the baking powder. Sift onto a large piece of parchment or wax paper.

4. Place the eggs, sugar, buttermilk, corn syrup, and vanilla in a large bowl. Stir with a whisk until combined. Add the melted chocolate and stir to combine. Add 1 cup of the pecans and 1 cup of the walnuts, and stir to combine. Finally, add the sifted dry ingredients, and stir until the batter is thoroughly combined. Pour the batter into the prepared baking pan, spreading it evenly with a rubber spatula.

continued

5. Place on the center rack of the oven, and bake until a toothpick inserted in the center of the brownies comes out clean, about 45 minutes total (halfway through the baking time, move the pan to the top rack and rotate it 180 degrees). Remove the brownies from the oven, and cool in the pan at room temperature while preparing the ganache.

MAKE THE DARK CHOCOLATE GANACHE:

6. Place the unsweetened and semisweet chocolates in a medium heatproof bowl. Bring the cream to a boil in a small saucepan over medium heat. Pour the cream over the chocolate; stir with a whisk until smooth. Pour the ganache over the cooled brownies, and use a rubber spatula to spread it evenly over the entire surface. Sprinkle the remaining pecans and walnuts evenly over the ganache.

7. To firm the ganache enough to cut, refrigerate for 1 hour. Cut into 12 to 24 portions and serve.

THE CHEF'S TOUCH

The unsweetened chocolate in this recipe is responsible for the intensity of flavor that makes these brownies more suitable for the older kids on your list. These brownies are perfect to pick up at a party or to serve as a plated dessert; and, if you choose the latter, a large dollop or two of the "Sloshed Santa" Sauce (see Santa's Workshop, page 171) makes a very jolly complement.

If the brownies are reluctant to exit the pan, wrap the pan with a damp, hot towel for a few moments and the brownies should yield to the possibility of consumption. They're Nutty Chocolate Brownies will keep for a couple of days at room temperature stored in a tightly sealed plastic container. For longer storage (4 to 5 days), cover the brownies with plastic wrap or store in a tightly sealed plastic container in the refrigerator. For the best flavor, bring them to room temperature before serving.

christmas breakfast chocolate sour cream crumb cakes

MAKES 18 CAKES

Get your Christmas morning going in the right direction with these appetite-soothing, sour cream–enhanced, cinnamon and walnut crumb–topped chocolate cupcakes. What a way to start a special day!

CINNAMON WALNUT CRUMB TOPPING

½ cup all-purpose flour

⅓ cup walnut halves, toasted (see Techniques, page 192) and coarsely chopped

¼ cup tightly packed light brown sugar

4 tablespoons (½ stick) unsalted butter, cut into small pieces

⅛ teaspoon ground cinnamon

¼ teaspoon salt

CHOCOLATE SOUR CREAM BREAKFAST CAKE BATTER

1½ cups all-purpose flour

¼ cup unsweetened cocoa powder

1 teaspoon baking powder

1 teaspoon baking soda

½ teaspoon salt

1 cup granulated sugar

8 tablespoons (1 stick) unsalted butter, cut into 1-tablespoon pieces

2 large eggs

2 ounces semisweet baking chocolate, coarsely chopped and melted (see Techniques, page 191)

½ cup buttermilk

½ cup sour cream

1 teaspoon pure vanilla extract

MAKE THE CINNAMON WALNUT CRUMB TOPPING:

1. Place the flour, walnuts, brown sugar, butter, cinnamon, and salt in the bowl of a stand electric mixer fitted with a paddle. Mix on the lowest speed for 4 minutes, then mix on medium for 30 seconds, until the mixture is crumbly.

MAKE THE CHOCOLATE SOUR CREAM BREAKFAST CAKE BATTER:

2. Preheat the oven to 350°F. Line 18 muffin tin cups with ½-inch foil liners.

3. In a sifter, combine the flour, cocoa, baking powder, baking soda, and salt. Sift onto a large piece of parchment or wax paper.

4. Place the granulated sugar and butter in a clean bowl of a stand electric mixer fitted with a paddle. Mix on low for 1 minute, then beat on medium for 2 minutes, until soft. Stop and scrape down the sides of the bowl and the paddle. Add the eggs, one at a time, beating on medium for 30 seconds after each addition, and scraping down again once the eggs have been incorporated (at this point the batter will look curdled; but don't worry, the melted chocolate will remedy the situation).

continued

5. Add the melted chocolate and mix on medium for 15 seconds. Scrape down again. Add the buttermilk and sour cream and beat on medium for 1 minute, until the mixture is thoroughly combined and smooth. Scrape down again. Turn on the mixer at the lowest speed and gradually add the dry ingredients; mix until incorporated, about 1 minute. Scrape down again. Add the vanilla and mix on medium to combine, about 15 seconds. Remove the bowl from the mixer, and use a rubber spatula to finish mixing the ingredients until thoroughly combined.

6. Portion 2 heaping tablespoons or 1 level #20 ice-cream scoop of batter into each muffin cup. Sprinkle 1 slightly heaping tablespoon of the Cinnamon Walnut Crumb Topping over as much of each cup of batter as possible. Place the muffin tins on the top and center racks of the oven, and bake until a toothpick inserted in the center of one of the cakes comes out ever so slightly moist with batter, about 20 minutes. (Switch the pans between top and center halfway through the baking time and rotate each 180 degrees.) Remove from the oven and cool at room temperature in the tins for 15 minutes. Remove the crumb cakes from the muffin tins (but not from the liners). Serve immediately, while still warm.

THE CHEF'S TOUCH

If these mini cakes remind you of streusel-covered coffee cakes, you're right. Streusel, which in German means "sprinkle," is a delightful topping for many goodies. With eighteen of these cakes, you can sprinkle them around and have quite a party.

Although best when served warm from the oven, the Christmas Breakfast Chocolate Sour Cream Crumb Cakes may be cooled to room temperature and stored for up to 48 hours at room temperature in a tightly sealed plastic container. The cakes may be warmed in a 250°F oven for a few moments; don't microwave them or they will acquire an unpleasant texture. Or just eat them at room temperature, and I can assuredly say pleasant Christmas memories will follow.

chocolate almond brown sugar cake

SERVES 10

Brown sugar, how come you taste so good? The answer is obvious once you taste this sublime composition of delicate golden brown sugar cake and bold chocolate buttercream. Just like a brown sugar cake should. Uh-huh.

GOLDEN ALMOND BROWN SUGAR CAKE

8 ounces (2 sticks) unsalted butter, cut into 1-tablespoon pieces, plus 1 tablespoon, melted

2 cups all-purpose flour

2 teaspoons baking powder

½ teaspoon salt

1½ cups tightly packed light brown sugar

3 large eggs

¼ cup whole milk

1 cup sliced almonds, toasted (see Techniques, page 192)

1 teaspoon pure vanilla extract

CHOCOLATE AMARETTO BUTTERCREAM

22 ounces semisweet baking chocolate, coarsely chopped

1 cup heavy cream

½ cup granulated sugar

¼ cup amaretto

1 pound (4 sticks) unsalted butter, cut into 1-tablespoon pieces and softened

GARNISH

14 to 16 whole toasted almonds

MAKE THE GOLDEN ALMOND BROWN SUGAR CAKE:

1. Preheat the oven to 350°F. Lightly coat two 9 × 1½–inch cake pans with some of the melted 1 tablespoon butter. Line the bottom of the pans with parchment or wax paper, then lightly coat the paper with more melted butter.

2. In a sifter, combine the flour, baking powder, and salt. Sift onto a large piece of parchment or wax paper.

3. Place the brown sugar and the remaining 8 ounces butter in the bowl of a stand electric mixer fitted with a paddle. Mix on the lowest speed for 1 minute, then beat on medium for 1 minute, until soft. Stop and scrape down the sides of the bowl. Beat on medium-high for 2 minutes, until very soft. Scrape down again. Add the eggs, one at a time, beating on medium for 30 seconds after each addition, and scrape down again once all the eggs have been incorporated. Beat the mixture on medium for 30 seconds more.

4. Turn the mixer down to low and gradually add half of the dry ingredients; mix until incorporated, about 45 seconds. Very gradually add the milk and mix to incorporate, about 30 seconds. Gradually add the remaining dry ingredients and mix for 30 seconds. Add the almonds and vanilla and mix on medium for 15 seconds, until thoroughly incorporated. Remove the bowl from the mixer. Use a rubber spatula to finish mixing the ingredients until thoroughly combined. Immediately divide the batter between the two prepared cake pans, spreading it evenly. Bake on the center rack of the oven until a toothpick inserted in the center of each layer comes out clean, about 20 minutes. Remove from the oven, and cool in the pans for 5 minutes. Use a paring knife to cut between the cake and the inside edge of the pan and invert the cake layers onto parchment or wax paper–covered cake circles. Carefully peel the paper away from the bottom of each layer. Refrigerate the cake layers uncovered. If you will be finishing the cake the next day, let the layers cool to room temperature and cover each layer with plastic wrap before refrigerating.

MAKE THE CHOCOLATE AMARETTO BUTTERCREAM:

5. While the cake is chilling, place about three quarters (16 ounces) of the chocolate in a large, heatproof bowl.

6. Combine the cream, sugar, and amaretto in a small saucepan over medium-high heat. When hot, stir to dissolve the sugar. Bring to a boil. Pour the boiling mixture over the chocolate in the large bowl. Stir with a whisk until smooth. Pour the mixture (now ganache) onto a baking sheet with sides, and spread evenly with an icing spatula. Refrigerate for 20 minutes, until chilled but not solid.

7. Place the softened butter in the clean bowl of a stand electric mixer fitted with a paddle. Mix on low for 1 minute; increase the speed to medium and beat for 2 minutes. Stop and scrape down the sides of the bowl and the paddle. Beat on medium-high for 1 minute more, until very soft. Scrape down again. Add the chilled ganache and beat on medium for 30 seconds. Scrape down again. Now beat on medium for 30 seconds more, until thoroughly combined (if you are not tempted to taste the buttercream, you are hopelessly temperate). Transfer 4¼ cups of the buttercream to a large bowl, and add the remaining chopped chocolate; use a rubber spatula to fold the chocolate into the buttercream. Fit a pastry bag with a star tip, and fill with the remaining 1½ cups buttercream.

ASSEMBLE THE CAKE:

8. Remove the cake layers from the refrigerator. Use an icing spatula to spread 1½ cups of the buttercream from the bowl as evenly and smoothly as possible over the top and sides of one of the inverted cake layers (baked top down). Place the second inverted layer on the buttercream and gently press it into place. Spread the remaining buttercream from the bowl onto the top and sides of the cake. With the pastry bag, pipe a circle of 14 to 16 stars, each about 1 inch high and 1 inch wide and touching the next, along the outside edge of the top of the cake. Top each star with a whole almond. Refrigerate the cake for 2 hours before serving.

9. Heat the blade of a serrated knife under hot running water and wipe dry before cutting each slice. Keep the slices at room temperature for 15 to 20 minutes before serving.

THE CHEF'S TOUCH

This cake may be prepared over two days.

day 1: Bake the Golden Almond Brown Sugar Cake. Once cooled to room temperature, cover each layer with plastic wrap and refrigerate until the next day.

day 2: Make the Chocolate Amaretto Buttercream, then ice and assemble the cake as directed. Refrigerate the cake for 2 hours before slicing and serving.

If you have ample space, the cake layers may be frozen for up to 4 weeks (wrap the layers well with plastic wrap to prevent dehydration and to protect them from freezer odors). When you are ready to assemble the cake, for best results thaw the cake layers in the refrigerator for about 12 hours.

The assembled cake may be kept in the refrigerator for up to 3 days before serving. To guard the precious cake from invading odors, refrigerate it in a tightly sealed plastic container.

"old-fashioned" cranberry apple chocolate chip crumble

SERVES 8 TO 10

It's not possible to bumble this crumble. Just an oldfangled dessert that everyone loves, Cranberry Apple Chocolate Chip Crumble is easy to prepare and smells grand while it is baking. One caveat that is hard to obey: The crumble must cool after it exits the oven, no matter how appealing the aroma. It's just too darn hot, plus the pause before the plating allows the wonderful flavors to meld.

CRUMBLE SPRINKLES

½ cup all-purpose flour

6 tablespoons (¾ stick) cold unsalted butter

¼ cup granulated sugar

¼ cup tightly packed light brown sugar

½ teaspoon ground cinnamon

CRUMBLE FILLING

4 tablespoons (½ stick) unsalted butter, melted

¼ cup plus 3 tablespoons granulated sugar

2 medium Granny Smith apples

2 medium Red Delicious apples

1 cup fresh or frozen whole cranberries

1 cup semisweet chocolate chips

1 tablespoon freshly squeezed lemon juice

GARNISH

Unsweetened whipped cream or Vivacious Vanilla Ice Cream (see Santa's Workshop, page 181)

MAKE THE CRUMBLE SPRINKLES:

1. Place the flour, butter, sugars, and cinnamon in the bowl of a food processor fitted with a metal blade. Process for 45 seconds, until crumbly sprinkles are formed.

MAKE THE CRUMBLE FILLING:

2. Lightly coat an 8 × 8 × 2–inch baking dish (for this recipe I prefer ovenproof glass, but metal will work) with the melted butter. Sprinkle 3 tablespoons of the sugar into the dish and shake it around to coat the inside of the dish.

3. Peel, core, and quarter each apple, and slice each quarter into ½-inch-thick slices. Place the apple slices into a large nonreactive bowl. Add the cranberries, chocolate chips, the remaining ¼ cup sugar, and the lemon juice, and stir to combine. Cover the bowl with plastic wrap and refrigerate for 20 minutes (this will prevent the apples from discoloring and allows the flavor-enhancing juices to come out).

4. Meanwhile, preheat the oven to 350°F.

continued

5. Remove the Crumble Filling from the refrigerator; stir the mixture and pour it all, including the juices, into the prepared dish. Use a rubber spatula to press the mixture down as evenly as possible into the dish. Scatter the Crumble Sprinkles evenly over the top. Bake on the center rack of the oven for 40 minutes (rotate the pan 180 degrees halfway through the baking time), until the filling is bubbling around the sides and the topping is light golden brown. Remove from the oven and set aside for 15 to 20 minutes before serving (it is too hot to eat before that).

6. Portion the desired amount (remember, it is fruit, so no need to be anything but generous) onto the serving plates or bowls, and serve warm with clouds of unsweetened whipped cream or with a generous scoop of the Vivacious Vanilla Ice Cream.

THE CHEF'S TOUCH

Although a crumble may fly under other banners—buckle, cobbler, grunt, and slump, just to name a few—it truly is a classic and much beloved dessert. A crumble always has a top but no bottom! Raw fruit, butter, and sugar to get the fruit juices flowing, and for this book, the addition of chocolate. How could you get into a slump with that mix?

For a change in the mix, consider fresh pears rather than apples.

If any of the crumble remains uneaten (oh, dear), it may be covered with plastic wrap and refrigerated for up to 3 days. Heat before serving.

ma tante minnie's chocolate peanut butter blossoms

MAKES SIXTEEN TO EIGHTEEN 2½-INCH BLOSSOMS

Here we come a-blossoming with a cookie-candy that is guaranteed to elicit smiles and an eruption of delight. The Blossom's delicate nature should not inhibit your approach to this cookie—the full reward lies in eating the cookie and imbedded candy simultaneously.

1¾ cups all-purpose flour

8 tablespoons (1 stick) unsalted butter, cut into 1-tablespoon pieces and softened

4 ounces semisweet baking chocolate, coarsely chopped

1 cup granulated sugar

½ cup creamy peanut butter

1 large egg

2 tablespoons whole milk

1 teaspoon baking soda

1 teaspoon pure vanilla extract

½ teaspoon salt

16 to 18 Reese's® Miniature Milk Chocolate Peanut Butter Cups®, unwrapped

1. Preheat the oven to 375°F. Line 2 baking sheets with parchment or wax paper.

2. Place the flour, butter, chocolate, ½ cup of the sugar, the peanut butter, egg, milk, baking soda, vanilla, and salt in the bowl of a stand electric mixer fitted with a paddle. Mix on low for 1 minute, until combined. Stop and scrape down the sides of the bowl and the paddle, then beat on medium for 10 seconds, until a dough forms (it does not take very long) and comes off the bottom of the bowl. Remove the bowl from the mixer. (At this point you will notice this dense dough exudes an amazingly seductive aroma of peanut butter and chocolate, giving you an indication of the good things to come. But due to the presence of raw egg in the dough, please refrain from nibbling any.)

3. Portion 3 level tablespoons or 1 level #50 ice-cream scoop of the dough for each Blossom. Use your hands to form each portion into a smooth ball. Roll the balls in the remaining ½ cup sugar, lightly coating each.

4. Place the balls on the baking sheets, about 4 inches apart widthwise and 2 inches apart lengthwise. Place the baking sheets on the top and center racks of the oven and bake for 10 minutes, until light golden brown, switching the sheets between top and center and rotating each 180 degrees halfway through the baking time.

continued

5. Remove from the oven and immediately top each Blossom with a peanut butter cup, pressing down so the cup is positioned about halfway into the cookie and creates cracks around the edges (it now resembles a flower blossom). Cool on the baking sheet until room temperature. Store in a tightly sealed plastic container.

THE CHEF'S TOUCH

My sweet aunt (*tante* in French) Minnie lived with her family in an apartment above ours, in the house my mother—Tante Minnie's sister—owns and has lived in for the last fifty-six years in Woonsocket, Rhode Island. Tante Minnie, her husband, and four children moved to my mom's house shortly after my dad passed away just before Christmas in 1955. It was a sad Christmas for the Desaulniers family, but one item brought much needed smiles: Tante Minnie's Peanut Butter Blossoms.

Back in those days in Woonsocket, Tante Minnie's Blossoms were festooned with a chocolate kiss rather than a peanut butter cup. Try them either way!

Ma Tante Minnie's Chocolate Peanut Butter Blossoms will stay fresh in a tightly sealed plastic container at room temperature for 5 to 6 days, or in the refrigerator for a week to 10 days (bring the cookies to room temperature before eating). I don't recommend freezing the Blossoms.

hungarian chocolate walnut roll

SERVES 10

You'll like getting "Nuttin' for Christmas" as long as the nuttin' is the nuts from our Hungarian Chocolate Walnut Roll. The tender pastry of this confection enrobes a filling that bursts with chocolate and walnuts. The sensation that you have eaten liquid fudge will have your mouth feeling chocolaty good.

TENDER PASTRY DOUGH

4 tablespoons (½ stick) unsalted butter, cut into 1-tablespoon pieces

¼ cup whole milk

1 large egg, whisked

4 teaspoons active dry yeast

¼ cup granulated sugar

Pinch of salt

1½ cups all-purpose flour, sifted, plus 2 tablespoons

LIQUID FUDGE FILLING

1 cup granulated sugar

7 tablespoons whole milk

2 large egg yolks, whisked

¼ teaspoon salt

1½ cups walnut halves, toasted (see Techniques, page 192) and finely chopped

6 ounces semisweet baking chocolate, coarsely chopped

¼ cup all-purpose flour

GARNISH

Vivacious Vanilla Ice Cream (see Santa's Workshop, page 181) or unsweetened whipped cream

MAKE THE TENDER PASTRY DOUGH:

1. Melt the butter in a medium saucepan over medium-low heat; remove from the heat. Add the milk and ¼ cup water and stir to combine. Keep the mixture at or below 110°F; otherwise, it will kill the yeast. Add the egg and yeast and stir with a whisk until the yeast has mostly dissolved. Add the sugar and salt and stir until the sugar has dissolved. Add the 1½ cups flour, and stir with a rubber spatula until a dough forms.

2. Lightly flour your hands and a clean, dry work surface with some of the remaining 2 tablespoons flour. Transfer the dough to the work surface. Knead the dough into a smooth ball, flouring your hands as necessary to prevent the dough from sticking; this should take no more than 40 seconds or so. Place the dough in a medium bowl and cover with a clean towel or plastic wrap. Refrigerate for 1½ hours, until the dough has doubled in volume.

MAKE THE LIQUID FUDGE FILLING:

3. Place the sugar, 6 tablespoons of the milk, the egg yolks, and salt in a large bowl. Whisk to combine. Use a rubber spatula to fold in the chopped walnuts, then the chocolate.

ASSEMBLE THE NUT ROLL:

4. Preheat the oven to 350°F. Place an 18 × 18–inch sheet of aluminum foil on a flat work surface. Lightly flour the foil with some of the ¼ cup of flour.

continued

5. Remove the dough from the refrigerator and uncover. Place the dough on the foil. Dust a rolling pin with some of the flour and roll the dough into a 16 × 10–inch rectangle about ⅛ inch thick. Pour the filling onto the dough, and use a rubber spatula to spread it to within 1 to 1½ inches from the edges. Begin rolling the dough; start with the longer side and roll away from you. Make a tight roll and pinch the ends as you roll to prevent the filling from squirting out. Continue to roll to the opposite end, then tuck each end under the roll. Transfer the dough by lifting the sheet of foil onto a baking sheet. Fold any excess foil under the baking sheet. Cover the dough with a clean towel or plastic wrap and let sit at room temperature for 20 minutes.

6. Use a pastry brush to lightly brush the dough with some of the remaining 1 tablespoon milk. Bake on the center rack of the oven for 30 minutes, until light golden brown (rotate the baking sheet 180 degrees halfway through the baking time). Remove from the oven, and cool at room temperature for 20 to 30 minutes.

7. Use a serrated knife to cut the nut roll into 1¼-inch-thick slices. Serve immediately with a scoop of Vivacious Vanilla Ice Cream or with unsweetened whipped cream.

THE CHEF'S TOUCH

Walnuts need not have an exclusive with this dessert. Pecans, hazelnuts, and even rich macadamia nuts would each lend their own specific character. A mix of nuts would create a delightful concert of nuttiness.

The reason for rolling out the pastry dough on a sheet of aluminum foil is twofold: First, it makes it easy to transfer the dough from the work surface to the baking sheet. Also, since the filling may ooze out of the dough, the foil makes cleaning easier.

Individually wrapped slices of Hungarian Chocolate Walnut Roll may be kept in a tightly sealed plastic container at room temperature for 2 to 3 days. The sliced nut roll can be stored for up to 1 week in the refrigerator. It is best eaten warm, so heat the slices in a 300°F oven for a few minutes before serving. You can also heat the slices individually in a microwave oven. Times will vary depending upon the wattage and power settings of your microwave oven; don't overdo it—ours were perfect after only 10 seconds.

beth's mocha madness cookies

MAKES THIRTY-TWO 3-INCH COOKIES

Warning: The chocolate and energizing espresso punch of Mocha Madness Cookies may enable you to fly with Santa and his reindeer.

MOCHA MADNESS COOKIES

2¾ cups all-purpose flour

1 teaspoon baking soda

1 teaspoon salt

8 ounces (2 sticks) unsalted butter, cut into 1-tablespoon pieces and softened

1 cup tightly packed dark brown sugar

2 large eggs

3 ounces semisweet baking chocolate, melted (see Techniques, page 191)

¼ teaspoon instant espresso powder, dissolved in 2 tablespoons warm water

2 teaspoons pure vanilla extract

8 ounces dark chocolate–covered espresso beans, coarsely chopped (1½ cups)

GARNISH

4 ounces semisweet baking chocolate, melted

MAKE THE MOCHA MADNESS COOKIES:

1. Preheat the oven to 325°F. Line 3 baking sheets with parchment or wax paper.

2. In a sifter, combine the flour, baking soda, and salt. Sift onto a large piece of parchment or wax paper.

3. Place the butter and sugar in the bowl of a stand electric mixer fitted with a paddle. Mix on medium for 2 minutes, then stop and scrape down the sides of the bowl and the paddle. Mix again on medium for 2 minutes, then scrape down again. Add the eggs one at a time and mix on medium until incorporated, about 30 seconds. Scrape down again. Add the melted chocolate and beat on medium for 15 seconds, until incorporated.

4. Turn the mixer down to the lowest speed and gradually add the dry ingredients; mix until incorporated, about 1 minute. Add the dissolved espresso and vanilla, and mix on low until thoroughly combined. Remove the bowl from the mixer, add the espresso beans, and use a rubber spatula to finish mixing the ingredients until thoroughly combined.

5. Using 3 slightly heaping tablespoons or 1 level #20 ice-cream scoop, portion 10 or 11 cookies on each baking sheet, spaced about 5 inches apart widthwise and 2 inches apart lengthwise. Place the baking sheets on the top and center racks of the oven, and bake for 12 minutes, switching the sheets between top and center racks and rotating each sheet

180 degrees halfway through the baking. Remove from the oven and cool the cookies on the baking sheets for 5 minutes. Transfer the cookies to a cooling rack and cool to room temperature. Repeat with the remaining cookie dough, as necessary, once the baking sheets cool (hold the dough at room temperature).

6. Once the cookies have cooled to room temperature, use a teaspoon to drizzle thin lines of melted chocolate in a zigzag fashion over the tops. Refrigerate for a few minutes to set the chocolate before serving. Store the cookies in a tightly sealed plastic container. These cookies will stay fresh in a tightly sealed plastic container at room temperature for 5 to 6 days or in the refrigerator for a week to 10 days (bring the cookies to room temperature before eating). The cookies may also be frozen in a tightly sealed plastic container for several weeks. Thaw the frozen cookies at room temperature before serving. If you freeze the cookies, apply the drizzle after the cookies have thawed.

THE CHEF'S TOUCH

The inspiration for this cookie came our way thanks to Beth Armstrong of Marlborough, Massachusetts. An enthusiastic lover of all things made with chocolate, Beth purchased my book, *Death by Chocolate Cookies*, with my e-mail address. She e-mailed me to compliment me on the book, and we have been trading chocolate talk via the Internet ever since.

Look for instant espresso powder at your local supermarket in the same general location as you find instant coffee; if espresso powder is unavailable, substitute instant coffee.

golly polly's doodles

MAKES SEVENTEEN 1½-INCH ROUND COOKIES

A funny-looking ping pong ball–shaped cookie with a funny name, Golly Polly's Doodles classically and blissfully combine chocolate and peanut butter. This delight will make you want to eat Golly Polly's Doodles all day.

DOODLE DOUGH

1½ cups all-purpose flour

½ cup unsweetened cocoa powder

½ teaspoon baking powder

½ teaspoon salt

8 tablespoons (1 stick) unsalted butter, cut into 1-tablespoon pieces and softened

¾ cup granulated sugar

¼ cup creamy peanut butter

1 large egg

1 teaspoon pure vanilla extract

DOODLE FILLING

¼ cup creamy peanut butter

¼ cup confectioners' sugar

MAKE THE DOODLE DOUGH:

1. Preheat the oven to 375°F. Line a baking sheet with parchment or wax paper.

2. In a sifter, combine the flour, cocoa, baking powder, and salt. Sift onto a large piece of parchment or wax paper.

3. Place the softened butter, ¼ cup of the granulated sugar, and the ¼ cup peanut butter in the bowl of a stand electric mixer fitted with a paddle. Mix on low for 1 minute, then on medium for 1 minute more. Stop and scrape down the sides of the bowl and the paddle. Mix on medium-high for 1 minute. Scrape down again.

4. Add the egg and vanilla and beat on medium for 30 seconds; scrape down again once they have been incorporated. Turn the mixer down to low and gradually add the dry ingredients; mix until incorporated, about 30 seconds. Remove the bowl from the mixer, and use a rubber spatula or your hands to finish mixing the ingredients until thoroughly combined. Chill the dough in the refrigerator while making the filling. (Do not keep the dough in the refrigerator for more than 20 minutes; otherwise, the dough will be difficult to form into the desired shape.)

MAKE THE DOODLE FILLING:

5. Place the ¼ cup peanut butter and the confectioners' sugar in a clean bowl of a stand electric mixer fitted with a paddle. Mix on low for 20 seconds, then beat on medium for 10 seconds. Remove the bowl from the mixer, and use a rubber spatula to finish mixing until the ingredients are thoroughly combined. Portion 17 level teaspoons of the filling onto a piece of parchment or wax paper. Roll each portion into a smooth, round ball.

continued

6. Using 1 heaping tablespoon or 1 level #50 ice-cream scoop, portion 17 pieces of dough. Roll each portion of dough into a smooth round ball, then flatten each ball in the palm of your hand into a 3-inch-diameter circle. Using your thumb, make a small indentation in the center of the dough. Place a filling ball in the indentation, then fold the dough around the filling and roll it into a smooth, round ball. Roll the balls in the remaining ¼ cup granulated sugar to lightly coat.

7. Place the Doodles on the prepared baking sheet about 1 inch apart widthwise and 2 inches apart lengthwise. Bake on the center rack of the preheated oven for 6 minutes (that's right—just 6 minutes), until barely firm. (Overbaking will cause these cookies to become hard.) Remove the cookies from the oven and transfer to a wire rack to cool to room temperature. Store in a tightly sealed plastic container.

THE CHEF'S TOUCH

Indiana-born Polly Conway served a four-month externship at the Trellis while she was a student majoring in baking and pastry at the Culinary Institute of America. The CIA is America's premiere college to learn the culinary arts. Although Polly is also a 1996 graduate of Indiana University with a degree in journalism, baking has been one of her passions since childhood. Polly developed the Doodles when she was in high school, and her family likes them so well that it is their cookie of choice for the holidays. I'll wager that many more outstanding cookie recipes will be just a part of Polly's baking legacy.

An alternative to the ball shape is to slightly flatten the Doodles with the bottom of a glass. Same exceptional cookie, but not quite as doodly.

Keep the Doodles in a tightly sealed plastic container, at room temperature, for 7 to 10 days. They may also be stored in the refrigerator for up to 2 weeks (bring them to room temperature before eating).

These Doodles are made for walking, so do not hesitate to ship them to your friends around the country as Polly does every holiday season. For maximum freshness, I suggest placing the Doodles in tightly closed resealable plastic bags before packing them in a shipping container.

the stoner family's cocoa coconut cake with warm dark chocolate fudge sauce

SERVES 12

To say this cake is moist is like saying there's snow at the North Pole. Flavored with cocoa and coconut and bathed with an Almond Coconut Syrup, the cake alone is heavenly. But wait, there's more—the Dark Chocolate Fudge Sauce is truly the icing on the cake, and you don't want to miss it.

ALMOND COCONUT SYRUP

4 tablespoons granulated sugar

½ teaspoon almond extract

½ teaspoon coconut extract

COCOA COCONUT CAKE

8 ounces (2 sticks) unsalted butter, cut into 1-tablespoon pieces and softened, plus 1 tablespoon, melted

2 cups plus 2 tablespoons all-purpose flour

½ cup unsweetened cocoa powder

1½ teaspoons baking powder

1 teaspoon salt

2 cups granulated sugar

5 large eggs

1 cup buttermilk

7 ounces (1 cup minus 2 tablespoons) canned coconut milk

1 tablespoon coconut extract

DARK CHOCOLATE FUDGE SAUCE

¾ cup heavy cream

4 ounces semisweet baking chocolate, coarsely chopped

2 ounces unsweetened baking chocolate, coarsely chopped

2 tablespoons unsalted butter

GARNISH

Vivacious Vanilla Ice Cream (see Santa's Workshop, page 181) or unsweetened whipped cream

MAKE THE ALMOND COCONUT SYRUP:

1. Combine the granulated sugar, 2 tablespoons water, and the almond and coconut extracts in a small saucepan over medium heat. Stir to dissolve the sugar. Remove from the heat and set aside.

MAKE THE COCOA COCONUT CAKE:

2. Preheat the oven to 325°F. Lightly coat a 13 × 9 × 2–inch nonstick baking pan with the melted 1 tablespoon butter. Flour the pan with the 2 tablespoons flour. Shake out the excess.

3. In a sifter, combine the remaining 2 cups flour, the cocoa, baking powder, and salt. Sift onto a large piece of parchment or wax paper.

continued

4. Place the sugar and remaining 8 ounces butter in the bowl of a stand electric mixer fitted with a paddle. Mix on low for 2 minutes, then beat on medium for 2 minutes. Stop and scrape down the sides of the bowl and the paddle. Beat for 1 minute more on medium-high, until softer and lighter in color. Scrape down again. Add the eggs one at a time, beating on medium for 30 seconds after each addition and scraping down again once all the eggs have been incorporated. Turn the mixer on to low and gradually add the dry ingredients; mix until incorporated, about 30 seconds. Scrape down again. Gradually add the buttermilk, followed by the coconut milk and coconut extract, and mix on low until incorporated, about 30 seconds. Remove the bowl from the mixer, and use a rubber spatula to finish mixing the batter until thoroughly combined. Transfer the batter to the prepared cake pan and spread evenly. Bake on the center rack of the oven until a toothpick inserted in the center of the cake comes out clean, about 55 minutes.

5. Remove the cake from the oven and cool in the pan at room temperature for 10 minutes. Use a pastry brush to brush about half the Almond Coconut Syrup over the entire top surface of the cake. Wait about 5 minutes, then brush the remaining syrup onto the cake.

MAKE THE DARK CHOCOLATE FUDGE SAUCE:

6. Heat the cream, chocolates, and butter in the top of a double boiler or in a medium glass bowl in a microwave oven (see Techniques, page 191), and stir until smooth.

7. Cut the cake into 12 servings. Serve each portion accompanied by warm Dark Chocolate Fudge Sauce and an ample scoop of Vivacious Vanilla Ice Cream or unsweetened whipped cream.

THE CHEF'S TOUCH

I have known Rod and Donna Stoner for more than forty years. Rod and I were classmates at the Culinary Institute of America from September 1963 until we graduated in June 1965. Both Rod and Donna hail from Mount Joy, Pennsylvania, where Rod's family operated a very successful catering business. You could say that Rod has been in the food business all of his life, culminating with a thirty-year stint at the Greenbrier Resort in White Sulphur Springs, West Virginia; he retired in 2006 as vice president of food and beverage for the Greenbrier Resort Management Company. Thank you, Rod and Donna, for sharing your recipe for this outstanding dessert.

If you have any Dark Chocolate Fudge Sauce left over (I won't believe it), you may refrigerate it in a tightly sealed plastic container. Cold sauce can be warmed in a double boiler or in a microwave oven.

Once cooled to room temperature, the Cocoa Coconut Cake may be refrigerated in a tightly sealed plastic container for 4 to 5 days. I enjoy this cake when it is cold, warm, or at room temperature. In other words, I like this cake anyway it comes, but don't forget the warm fudge sauce.

mrs. lenhardt's chocolate almond toffee

MAKES 2½ POUNDS

Santa Claus is coming to town to get Mrs. Lenhardt's Chocolate Almond Toffee! Thick and crunchy, covered with chocolate and almonds, this toffee is irresistible to the big guy in the red suit and everyone on his list.

2¼ cups granulated sugar

8 ounces (2 sticks) unsalted butter, cut into 1-tablespoon pieces

2 tablespoons light corn syrup

2 cups whole almonds, toasted (see Techniques, page 192), each cut in half

4 ounces semisweet baking chocolate, melted (see Techniques, page 191)

1. Combine the sugar, butter, ½ cup water, and the corn syrup in a large saucepan over medium heat. Stir to dissolve the sugar and melt the butter. Bring to a boil, stirring only once or twice to prevent sticking and burning (frequent stirring causes the toffee to crystallize), and continue to cook until the mixture reaches a temperature of 360°F and becomes dark caramel in color, about 12 minutes. Use a digital thermometer (see Equipment, page 186) for an accurate temperature reading of the mixture.

2. Remove from the heat and wait about 10 seconds for the bubbles in the mixture to dissipate, then use a heat-resistant silicone spatula to fold in 1 cup of the almonds. Pour the mixture into a baking sheet with sides, and use the spatula to spread the mixture evenly. Cool the toffee at room temperature for 10 minutes, then refrigerate for 20 minutes.

3. Remove the toffee from the refrigerator. Use an offset spatula (see Equipment, page 186) to spread the melted chocolate over the surface of the toffee, then sprinkle the remaining cup of almond pieces over the surface of the melted chocolate. Refrigerate the toffee for about 30 minutes, until hard, then break into pieces. Store in a tightly sealed plastic container.

THE CHEF'S TOUCH

Trellis pastry chef Heather Lenhardt, a Johnson and Wales University graduate, shared the recipe for her mom's toffee, which was famous among her fourteen children and anyone else who was lucky enough to enjoy it. Even with a passel of kids running around the Lenhardt home, Heather's mom saved time to make—and to train Heather to create—this delicious confection.

As with similar candies, the key factor in successful toffee making is the temperature. I highly recommend using a digital thermometer (see Equipment, page 186) or a candy thermometer. Using the cooking time alone renders the candy making an iffy proposition.

Chocolate Almond Toffee can be stored for 2 to 3 weeks at room temperature in a tightly sealed plastic container; the shininess of the chocolate will diminish over time, but the toffee will still be delicious. You may also freeze the toffee; thaw at room temperature before eating.

HOME

baby, it's cold outside

chocolate espresso frenzy ice cream

MAKES 1¼ QUARTS

See photo, page 46

Yikes! If you eat this ice cream before Santa arrives, you'll have the energy to shimmy back up the chimney with him. This is caffeine at its finest. Chocolate Espresso Frenzy is a mocha ice cream blend of semisweet chocolate and espresso, peppered with shards of unsweetened chocolate. No long winter's nap for you—just the yin and yang and "YOW!" that will never be achieved at your local coffee shop.

2 cups heavy cream

1½ cups half-and-half

1 cup granulated sugar

2 tablespoons instant espresso powder

3 large eggs

8 ounces semisweet baking chocolate, coarsely chopped

4 ounces unsweetened baking chocolate, coarsely chopped

1. Combine the heavy cream, half-and-half, ½ cup of the sugar, and the espresso powder in a large saucepan over medium heat. Bring to a boil (5 to 6 minutes), stirring to dissolve the sugar. Remove from the heat.

2. Place the remaining ½ cup sugar and the eggs in a medium bowl. Whisk until thoroughly combined. Ladle ½ cup of the hot cream, 2 tablespoons at a time, into the eggs and whisk gently to incorporate.

3. Pour the egg and cream mixture into the saucepan and whisk until thoroughly combined. Cook over medium heat, stirring constantly, until it reaches 185°F, about 2 minutes. Use a digital thermometer (see Equipment, page 186) for an accurate reading.

4. Remove from the heat, add the semisweet chocolate, and stir gently to melt the chocolate. Pour through a fine-gauge strainer into a large stainless-steel bowl. Place the bowl in an ice-water bath to cool the mixture to 40° to 45°F. When the mixture is cold, freeze in an ice-cream machine following the manufacturer's instructions.

5. Transfer the ice cream to a 2-quart plastic container. Use a rubber spatula to fold in the unsweetened chocolate until evenly distributed. Securely cover the container and place in the freezer for several hours before serving.

THE CHEF'S TOUCH

At the Trellis, we use Ferrara® instant espresso powder. You can find this product at your local supermarket where you find instant coffee. If espresso powder is unavailable, you may substitute an equal amount of instant coffee.

Chocolate Espresso Frenzy Ice Cream is best served within 5 to 6 days of preparation. Keep the container of ice cream securely covered in the freezer to prevent the ice cream from dehydrating and absorbing freezer odors.

eggnog chocolate fudge swirl ice cream

MAKES 1½ QUARTS

Luscious frozen eggnog could change holiday traditions forever. Like its drinkable counterpart, this ice cream is a rich experience with provocative trade-offs: a bowl and a spoon instead of a cup, rich fudge swirl instead of the ticklish spray of nutmeg, and plenty of real heavy cream and egg yolks instead of the foamy, thickened substance found in commercial eggnog. Tra-la-la-la-la!

CHOCOLATE FUDGE SWIRL

⅓ cup heavy cream

⅓ cup tightly packed dark brown sugar

⅓ cup granulated sugar

2 teaspoons unsalted butter, melted

Dash of salt

½ cup unsweetened cocoa powder, sifted

EGGNOG ICE CREAM

2 cups heavy cream

1½ cups half-and-half

¾ cup granulated sugar

3 large egg yolks

4 tablespoons brandy

MAKE THE FUDGE SWIRL:

1. Combine the heavy cream, sugars, melted butter, and salt in a small saucepan over medium-high heat. Bring to a boil (less than a minute), stirring to dissolve the sugars. Remove from the heat and slowly whisk in the cocoa. Continue to whisk until the lumps have been eliminated. Pour the fudge into a medium stainless-steel bowl. Place the bowl in an ice-water bath to cool the fudge to 40° to 45°F.

MAKE THE EGGNOG ICE CREAM:

2. Combine the heavy cream, half-and-half, and ½ cup of the sugar in a large saucepan over medium heat. Stir to dissolve the sugar. Bring to a boil, stirring to dissolve the sugar (5 to 6 minutes), then remove from the heat.

3. Place the remaining ¼ cup sugar and the egg yolks in a medium bowl. Whisk until thoroughly combined. Ladle ½ cup of the hot cream, 2 tablespoons at a time, into the eggs and whisk gently to incorporate. Pour the egg and cream mixture into the saucepan and whisk until thoroughly combined. Cook over medium heat, stirring constantly, until it reaches 185°F, about 1 minute. Use a digital thermometer (see Equipment, page 186) for an accurate reading.

4. Remove from the heat. Pour the mixture through a fine-gauge strainer into a large stainless-steel bowl. Place the bowl in an ice-water bath to cool the mixture to 40° to 45°F.

continued

5. When the mixture is cold, add the brandy and stir gently to incorporate. Freeze in an ice-cream machine following the manufacturer's instructions.

6. Transfer the ice cream to a 2-quart plastic container. Use a rubber spatula to swirl in the fudge. Securely cover the container, then place in the freezer for several hours before serving.

THE CHEF'S TOUCH

Although there is an eggnoglike liqueur called *advocaat*, produced in Europe, the tradition of drinking eggnog at Christmastime is an American one. I was never fond of the nonalcoholic dairy beverage offered to me as a youngster, but as an adult I became enamored with a brandy-laced drink I would often pair with a piece of fudge. Well, here it is—all in one! Out of brandy? Rum makes an agreeable alternative.

Eggnog Chocolate Fudge Swirl Ice Cream is best served within 5 to 6 days of preparation. Keep the container of ice cream securely covered in the freezer to prevent the ice cream from dehydrating and absorbing freezer odors.

white chocolate cinnamon cherrylicious ice cream

MAKES 1½ QUARTS

A bowl of this ice cream is as smile-inducing as a colorfully decorated Christmas tree. It's actually better, because you can eat the ice cream. The tingling bite of the cinnamon liqueur plays off the velvety texture of the white chocolate ice cream, which is bedecked with maraschino cherries like a bunch of presents. We wish you a Cherry Christmas.

8 ounces white chocolate, coarsely chopped

1½ cups half-and-half

2 cups heavy cream

¾ cup granulated sugar

3 large eggs

2 tablespoons AfterShock® Hot & Cool Cinnamon Liqueur

1 cup drained, stemmed maraschino cherries (about 30 cherries), coarsely chopped

1. Melt the chocolate in ½ cup of the half-and-half in the top of a double boiler or in a medium glass bowl in a microwave oven (see Techniques, page 191) and stir until smooth.

2. Bring the heavy cream and the remaining 1 cup half-and-half with ¼ cup of the sugar to a boil in a large saucepan over medium heat, stirring to dissolve the sugar, 5 to 6 minutes. Remove from the heat.

3. Place the remaining ½ cup sugar and the eggs in a medium bowl. Whisk until thoroughly combined. Ladle ½ cup of the hot cream, 2 tablespoons at a time, into the eggs and whisk gently to incorporate.

4. Pour the egg and cream mixture back into the saucepan and whisk until thoroughly combined. Add the melted chocolate and whisk until combined. Cook over medium heat, stirring constantly, until it reaches 185°F, 2 to 3 minutes. Use a digital thermometer (see Equipment, page 186) for an accurate reading. Pour through a fine-gauge strainer into a large stainless-steel bowl. Place the bowl in an ice-water bath to cool the mixture to 40° to 45°F. Add the AfterShock and stir gently to combine. When the mixture is cold, freeze in an ice-cream machine following the manufacturer's instructions.

5. Transfer the ice cream to a 2-quart plastic container. Use a rubber spatula to fold in the chopped maraschino cherries until evenly distributed. Securely cover the container, then place in the freezer for several hours before serving.

THE CHEF'S TOUCH

With just 2 tablespoons of cinnamon liqueur distributed into 1½ quarts of ice cream, even Santa Claus would agree that this delightful confection can be enjoyed by children of all ages. Of course it may be omitted, but so can Santa's visit to your house.

I enjoy the distinctive cinnamon-flavored bite imparted by the AfterShock Hot & Cool Cinnamon Liqueur. If you are not able to locate this particular liqueur, an acceptable substitute would be cinnamon schnapps (in that genre, check out Fire Water™ Hot Cinnamon Schnapps Liqueur).

This ice cream is best when served within 5 to 6 days of preparation. Keep the container of ice cream securely covered in the freezer to prevent the ice cream from dehydrating and absorbing freezer odors.

cranberry chocolate chip oatmeal cookie ice cream terrine

SERVES 8

Tra-la-la-la-la, just an old-fashioned ice-cream terrine! The cinnamon-enhanced ice cream, embellished by Cranberry Chocolate Chip Oatmeal Cookies and chocolate chunks, underscores our love affair with chocolate. Just an old-fashioned ice-cream terrine—one I'm sure they made for you and me.

1½ cups heavy cream

1½ cups half-and-half

½ cup granulated sugar

2 teaspoons pure vanilla extract

½ teaspoon ground cinnamon

3 Cranberry Chocolate Chip Oatmeal Cookies (see Been Nice Sweets, page 123), cut into ½-inch pieces

2 ounces semisweet baking chocolate, coarsely chopped

Vegetable pan spray

GARNISH

Dark Chocolate Fudge Sauce (see Home for the Holidays, page 41)

MAKE THE ICE CREAM:

1. Heat ½ cup of the heavy cream, ½ cup of the half-and-half, and the sugar in a small saucepan over medium heat, stirring to dissolve the sugar. Remove from the heat. The temperature should be about 125°F; use a digital thermometer (see Equipment, page 186) for an accurate reading. Transfer to a bowl. Add the remaining heavy cream and half-and-half, the vanilla, and the cinnamon, and stir with a whisk to incorporate. Place the bowl in an ice-water bath to cool to 40° to 45°F. Freeze in an ice-cream freezer following the manufacturer's instructions.

ASSEMBLE, FREEZE, AND SERVE THE TERRINE:

2. Transfer the ice cream to a large bowl. Use a rubber spatula to fold in the cookie pieces and the chocolate.

3. Lightly spray a 9 × 5 × 2½–inch loaf pan with vegetable pan spray, then line the pan with plastic wrap so that the wrap extends down over the sides of the pan.

4. Transfer the ice cream to the prepared pan, spreading evenly with a rubber spatula. Fold the plastic wrap up and over the ice cream, then tightly cover the wrap with aluminum foil. Freeze the terrine for at least 24 hours before serving. Serve within 5 to 6 days.

continued

5. To serve, remove the terrine from the freezer, and remove and discard the foil. Invert the frozen terrine (still in its plastic wrapping) onto a clean, dry cutting board. If the frozen terrine is reluctant to exit the terrine pan, wrap a damp, hot towel around the pan for a few seconds, and the frozen terrine should slip out easily. Remove and discard the plastic wrap. Slice the ends from the terrine (the ice-cream maker's reward?), and then cut the terrine into 8 slices about 1 inch thick. Heat the blade of a serrated knife under hot running water and wipe dry before making each slice.

6. Serve immediately on a plate generously sauced with Dark Chocolate Fudge Sauce.

THE CHEF'S TOUCH

Almost from day one—November 10, 1980—we have featured ice-cream terrines on the Trellis's Desserts To Die For® menu. Easy to prepare and serve, ice-cream terrines are a favorite, especially when enhanced with the textures and flavors we present in this terrine. If you don't feel like baking cookies—shame on you!—consider replacing the cookies with 1 cup chocolate chips and 1½ cups dried cranberries.

To prevent the terrine from dehydrating and absorbing freezer odors, keep it tightly wrapped while in the freezer. Ice cream terrine slices may be wrapped with plastic wrap and placed in a tightly sealed plastic container for several days.

frozen chocolate grasshopper pie

SERVES 8

Do you hear what I hear? A chocolate grasshopper pie in the freezer! Not the gelatin and whipped cream dessert of the 1950s, but a frozen pie brimming with chocolate and a heavenly crème de menthe ice cream. Now do you hear?

CHOCOLATE CHUNK CRÈME DE MENTHE ICE CREAM

3 cups heavy cream

¾ cup granulated sugar

1 vanilla bean, cut in half lengthwise

1½ teaspoons green crème de menthe

4 ounces semisweet baking chocolate, cut into ¼-inch pieces

DARK CHOCOLATE GANACHE

4 ounces semisweet baking chocolate, coarsely chopped

2 ounces unsweetened baking chocolate, coarsely chopped

1 cup heavy cream

GRASSHOPPER CHOCOLATE CHUNK COOKIE CRUST

1 teaspoon unsalted butter, melted

Flour, for kneading

Grasshopper Chocolate Chunk Cookies (see Santa's Workshop, page 176), unbaked

MAKE THE CHOCOLATE CHUNK CRÈME DE MENTHE ICE CREAM:

1. Heat 2 cups heavy cream, the sugar, and vanilla bean in a medium saucepan over medium heat. When hot, stir to dissolve the sugar, then remove from the heat (the temperature will be about 125°F). Add the remaining cup of cream and crème de menthe and stir to incorporate. Remove the vanilla bean, and then cool in an ice-water bath to a temperature of 40° to 45°F. Freeze in an ice-cream freezer following the manufacturer's instructions.

2. Transfer the semifrozen ice cream to a 2 quart plastic container. Use a rubber spatula to fold in the 4 ounces of chocolate chunks. Securely cover the container, then place in the freezer while making the ganache and the cookie crust.

PREPARE THE DARK CHOCOLATE GANACHE:

3. Place the chopped semisweet chocolate and the chopped unsweetened chocolate in a medium bowl. Heat the heavy cream in a small saucepan over medium heat. Bring to a boil. Pour the boiling cream over the chopped chocolate and stir with a whisk until smooth. Set aside at room temperature until needed.

PREPARE THE GRASSHOPPER CHOCOLATE CHUNK COOKIE CRUST:

4. Preheat the oven to 350°F. Lightly coat the insides of a 9 × 1½–inch pie pan with the teaspoon of melted butter. Set aside.

continued

5. Lightly flour a clean, dry work surface. Transfer half of the dough to the work surface (the remaining dough may be frozen or baked into cookies). Knead the dough into a ball. Place the ball in the buttered pie pan, and use your hands to spread the dough uniformly over the bottom and sides of the pan, including the top flat edge of the pan (the dough on the top flat edge will prevent the crust from sagging into the pan while baking).

6. Line the dough with aluminum foil, pressing the foil down gently into the dough with your hands, and then bake on the center rack of the oven for 10 minutes.

7. Remove the pan from the oven and remove and discard the foil. Use a fork to prick the bottom of the crust in several places. Return the pan to the oven and bake for an additional 8 minutes, until very light golden brown around the top edges of the crust. Remove from the oven and cool at room temperature for 20 minutes.

ASSEMBLE AND DECORATE THE PIE:

8. Place the frozen ice cream in the refrigerator to allow for smooth spreading in the baked cookie crust.

9. Once the crust has cooled to room temperature, pour ¾ cup of the ganache into the crust and use a rubber spatula to spread the ganache over the entire surface, bottom, and sides of the crust. Place the ganache-covered crust in the freezer to harden the ganache, 15 to 20 minutes.

10. Remove the crust from the freezer and fill with the ice cream, spreading evenly. Drizzle the remaining ganache in a zigzag pattern over the top of the ice cream. Return the pie to the freezer for several hours before serving.

11. To serve, remove the pie from the freezer. Wrap a damp, hot towel around the bottom of the pan for a few seconds to loosen the pie from the pan. Slide the pie out of the pan onto a clean, dry cutting board (if it does not slide out, wrap the hot towel around the bottom of the pan for a few more seconds). Heat the blade of a serrated knife under hot running water and wipe the blade dry before making each slice. I recommend keeping the slices at air-conditioned room temperature (70°F to no warmer than 76°F) for 20 to 30 minutes before serving. The frozen pie is too hard in texture to eat before that time and believe it or not, the pie will not melt even a drop. As a testament to the richness of the ice cream, I have experimented with holding the pie at room temperature for more than 1 hour, and still no melting!

THE CHEF'S TOUCH

Homemade grasshopper pie was a staple restaurant dessert in the days before the restaurant industry became institutionalized. In the typical chain restaurant today, your grasshopper pie probably rolls off the assembly line in a factory in Baltimore. Here we have incorporated the flavors of old in an updated combination. Wax nostalgic no more.

After assembly, you may keep the Frozen Chocolate Grasshopper Pie in the freezer for several days. To avoid permeating the pie with freezer odors, place the pie in a large, tightly sealed plastic container.

pumpkin pecan caramel chocolate fudge ice cream cake

SERVES 12

No, it's not a mirage. It's a tower of ice cream and cake, a fantasy of flavors, a tsunami of textures to tantalize your eyes and reward your mouth. Forget the presents this Christmas, just give me this pumpkin phantasmagoria.

PUMPKIN PECAN CARAMEL CHOCOLATE FUDGE ICE CREAM

1⅓ cups heavy cream

⅔ cup whole milk

⅔ cup granulated sugar

⅛ teaspoon ground nutmeg

4 large egg yolks

1 cup solid pack pumpkin

¼ cup bourbon

1 cup pecan halves, toasted (see Techniques, page 192), each half broken in 2 to 3 pieces

CHOCOLATE FUDGE SAUCE

2 ounces semisweet baking chocolate, coarsely chopped

1 ounce unsweetened baking chocolate, coarsely chopped

5 tablespoons heavy cream

1 tablespoon unsalted butter

CARAMEL SAUCE

⅓ cup heavy cream

1 tablespoon unsalted butter

3 tablespoons granulated sugar

2 drops freshly squeezed lemon juice

CHOCOLATE FUDGE CAKE

6 tablespoons (¾ stick) unsalted butter, cut into 1-tablespoon pieces and softened, plus 1 tablespoon, melted

1¼ cups all-purpose flour

1½ teaspoons baking soda

⅛ teaspoon salt

1¼ cups tightly packed light brown sugar

2 large eggs

2 ounces unsweetened baking chocolate, melted (see Techniques, page 191)

¾ cup sour cream

1 teaspoon pure vanilla extract

¾ cup Godiva Original Chocolate Liqueur

CHOCOLATE GANACHE

12 ounces semisweet baking chocolate, coarsely chopped

1 cup heavy cream

2 tablespoons unsalted butter

GARNISH

2 ½ cups pecan halves, toasted (see Techniques, page 192) and coarsely chopped

Pumpkin Spice Crème Anglaise (see Santa's Workshop, page 180)

MAKE THE PUMPKIN PECAN CARAMEL CHOCOLATE FUDGE ICE CREAM:

1. Bring the heavy cream, milk, ⅓ cup of the granulated sugar, and the nutmeg to a boil in a medium saucepan over medium-high heat, stirring to dissolve the sugar. Remove from the heat.

2. Place the egg yolks and the remaining ⅓ cup granulated sugar in a medium bowl. Whisk until thoroughly combined. Ladle ¾ cup of the hot cream, 2 tablespoons at a time, into the egg yolks and whisk gently to incorporate. Pour the egg yolk and cream mixture back into saucepan, and whisk until thoroughly combined. Cook over medium heat, stirring constantly, until it reaches 185°F, about 30 seconds. Use a digital thermometer (see Equipment, page 186) for an accurate reading.

3. Remove from the heat and pour through a fine-gauge strainer into a large stainless-steel bowl. Add the pumpkin and stir to combine. Place the bowl in an ice water bath to cool the mixture to 40° to 45°F.

4. When the mixture is cold, use a rubber spatula to fold in the bourbon and stir to combine. Freeze the mixture in an ice-cream freezer according to the manufacturer's instructions.

MAKE THE CHOCOLATE FUDGE SAUCE:

5. Heat the chocolates, heavy cream, and butter in the top of a double boiler or in a medium glass bowl in a microwave oven (see Techniques, page 191), and stir until smooth.

MAKE THE CARAMEL SAUCE:

6. Bring the heavy cream and butter to a simmer in a small saucepan over medium heat. Remove from the heat.

7. Place the granulated sugar and lemon juice in another small saucepan. Stir with a long-handled metal kitchen spoon to combine. (The sugar will resemble moist sand.) Cook the sugar over medium-high heat, stirring constantly to break up any lumps, for 2 minutes and 15 seconds; the sugar will first turn clear as it liquefies, then light brown as it caramelizes. Remove the saucepan from the heat. Carefully add the hot cream to the caramelized sugar, whisking vigorously with a 12-inch-long balloon whisk until the mixture stops bubbling. Transfer the sauce to a medium heatproof bowl. Allow to cool to room temperature.

FINISH THE ICE CREAM:

8. Transfer the ice cream to a 2-quart plastic container. Use a rubber spatula to fold in the pecan pieces. Add the Chocolate Fudge Sauce and use the spatula to give the mixture two folds. Add the Caramel Sauce and give the mixture 5 to 6 folds. Securely cover the container and place in the freezer until just before assembling the cake.

continued

MAKE THE CHOCOLATE FUDGE CAKE:

9. Preheat the oven to 325°F. Lightly coat three 9 × 1½–inch round cake pans with some of the 1 tablespoon melted butter. Line the bottom of the pans with parchment or wax paper, then lightly coat the paper with more melted butter.

10. In a sifter, combine the flour, baking soda, and salt. Sift onto a large piece of parchment or wax paper.

11. Place the 6 tablespoons butter and the brown sugar in the bowl of a stand electric mixer fitted with a paddle. Mix on low for 1 minute, then on medium for 2 minutes. Stop and scrape down the sides of the bowl and the paddle. Beat on medium-high for 1 minute, until very soft. Scrape down again. Add the eggs one at a time, beating on medium for 30 seconds after each addition and scraping down again once all of the eggs have been incorporated.

12. Add the melted chocolate and beat on medium for 30 seconds. Scrape down again. Turn the mixer on at low and gradually add the dry ingredients; mix until incorporated, about 30 seconds. Scrape down again. Add the sour cream and the vanilla, and mix on low for 15 seconds, until thoroughly combined. Gradually add the Godiva liqueur and mix on low for 15 seconds, then on medium for 15 seconds, until all the ingredients are blended. Remove the bowl from the mixer, and use a rubber spatula to finish mixing the batter until it is smooth and creamy.

13. Immediately divide the batter into the prepared pans, spreading evenly with a rubber spatula. Bake on the center rack of the oven until a toothpick inserted in the center of each layer comes out clean, about 15 minutes. Remove from the oven and cool in the pans at room temperature for 10 minutes. Invert the cake layers onto cake circles or cake plates. Carefully peel the paper from the bottom of each layer. Refrigerate the cake layers, uncovered, for at least 1 hour before assembly.

BEGIN TO ASSEMBLE THE ICE CREAM CAKE:

14. Wrap the bottom insert of a 9 × 2¾–inch nonstick springform pan with plastic wrap, then assemble the pan with the bottom insert turned over (the lip of the insert facing down).

15. Remove the cake layers from the refrigerator and the ice cream from the freezer. Turn one of the cake layers over (baked top up) and place it in the springform pan. Portion about half of the ice cream on top of the cake. Use a rubber spatula to spread the ice cream evenly over the cake to the edge of the pan. Turn another layer over and onto the ice cream in the pan, and gently press it into place. Spread the remaining ice cream evenly over the cake to the edge of the pan. Turn the last layer over and place on top of the ice cream. Cover the pan with plastic wrap and place in the freezer for at least 12 hours, until the ice cream cake is frozen solid.

MAKE THE CHOCOLATE GANACHE:

16. Just before finishing the cake, place the chocolate into a medium heatproof bowl. Bring the heavy cream and butter to a boil in a medium saucepan over medium-high heat. Pour the cream over the chocolate, and whisk until smooth and incorporated.

FINISH THE ASSEMBLY AND SERVE:

17. Remove the cake from the freezer. Release the cake from the springform pan and position it on a wire rack over a baking sheet with sides. Pour the ganache over the top of the cake, then use an icing spatula to spread the ganache smoothly and evenly over the top and sides of the cake. Use a utility turner to transfer the cake to a clean cake circle. Return the cake to the freezer for 15 minutes.

18. Remove the cake from the freezer. Press the chopped pecans into the sides of the ganache, coating the sides evenly. Return the cake to the freezer for another 30 minutes before slicing and serving.

19. To serve, heat the blade of a serrated knife under hot running water and wipe dry before cutting each slice. Serve immediately, accompanied by Pumpkin Spice Crème Anglaise.

THE CHEF'S TOUCH

I know what you're thinking. Believe me, this dessert is worth the trouble. It is much easier to remove the frozen cake from the bottom of the pan if you first turn it over (the lip facing down) and wrap it with plastic wrap before assembling the cake in the pan.

If the ice cream is too hard to spread evenly onto the cake layers, soften it in the refrigerator for about 45 minutes. Leave the cake layers in the refrigerator while the ice cream is softening.

After assembly, you may keep this cake in the freezer for several days. To prevent the cake from absorbing freezer odors, store it in a tightly sealed plastic container.

This cake may be prepared over 3 days:

day 1: Make and freeze the Pumpkin Pecan Caramel Chocolate Fudge Ice Cream. Bake the Chocolate Fudge Cake layers. Once cooled, cover each layer with plastic wrap and refrigerate until the next day.

day 2: Remove the cake layers from the refrigerator and the ice cream from the freezer. Assemble the cake layers in the springform pan as directed in the recipe. Cover with plastic wrap and freeze until final assembly.

day 3: Make the Chocolate Ganache. Pour the ganache over the cake. Return it to the freezer for 30 minutes before pressing the pecans into the sides of the cake, then return the cake to the freezer for 30 minutes more before slicing and serving.

chocolate drop peanut butter ice cream sandwiches

MAKES 10 SANDWICHES

Not your typical ice cream sandwich, it's a Chocolate Drop Peanut Butter Ice Cream Sandwich. The peanut butter is plentiful, the Godiva liqueur is sassy, and the ice cream wedged between ample Chocolate Drop Cookies is a blizzard of delight. Decoratively adorned with Chocolate Peanut Butter Ganache and chopped peanuts, the temptation to hang these sandwiches from the holiday tree is strong. But eating, rather than viewing, is this pleasure of the season (anyway, kinda messy—ice cream on the tree).

PEANUT BUTTER ICE CREAM

2 cups heavy cream

2 cups half-and-half

¾ cup creamy peanut butter, melted (see The Chef's Touch, page 66)

½ cup granulated sugar

1 vanilla bean, cut in half lengthwise

3 tablespoons Godiva Original Chocolate Liqueur

CHOCOLATE DROP COOKIES

2 cups all-purpose flour

⅔ cup unsweetened cocoa powder

1 teaspoon baking soda

½ teaspoon salt

1½ cups granulated sugar

8 ounces (2 sticks) unsalted butter, cut into 1-tablespoon pieces and softened

2 large eggs

1 teaspoon pure vanilla extract

CHOCOLATE PEANUT BUTTER GANACHE

4 ounces semisweet baking chocolate, coarsely chopped

½ cup creamy peanut butter

½ cup heavy cream

1 tablespoon granulated sugar

GARNISH

2½ cups unsalted dry roasted peanuts, coarsely chopped

MAKE THE PEANUT BUTTER ICE CREAM:

1. Combine the heavy cream, half-and-half, peanut butter, sugar, and vanilla bean in a medium saucepan over medium heat, stirring to dissolve the sugar and incorporate the peanut butter. Cook until it reaches 165°F, 4 minutes. Use a digital thermometer (see Equipment, page 186) for an accurate reading. Remove from the heat. (At this point the mixture does not have a homogenized appearance; that will come during the freezing process.) Pour into a medium stainless-steel bowl. Remove the vanilla bean.

2. Place the bowl in an ice-water bath to cool to 40° to 45°F. Add the Godiva liqueur and stir gently to combine. When the mixture is cold, freeze in an ice-cream machine following the manufacturer's instructions.

3. Transfer the ice cream to a 2-quart plastic container. Securely cover the container and place in the freezer for several hours.

MAKE THE CHOCOLATE DROP COOKIES:

4. Preheat the oven to 350°F. Line 4 baking sheets with parchment or wax paper.

5. In a sifter, combine the flour, cocoa, baking soda, and salt. Sift onto a large piece of parchment or wax paper.

6. Place the sugar and butter in the bowl of a stand electric mixer fitted with a paddle. Mix on low for 1 minute, then beat on medium for 1 minute. Stop and scrape down the sides of the bowl and the paddle. Beat on medium-high for 1 minute. Scrape down again. Add the eggs and vanilla and beat for 30 seconds on medium. Turn the mixer on to low and gradually add the dry ingredients; mix until incorporated, about 30 seconds. Remove the bowl from the mixer, and use a rubber spatula to finish mixing the dough until thoroughly combined (a little elbow grease will help, as the dough is quite stiff).

7. Using 2 heaping tablespoons or 1 level #20 ice-cream scoop, portion 5 cookies on each of the baking sheets, about 2½ inches apart widthwise and lengthwise. (Depending on your portioning precision, you may end up with an extra cookie for the baker's pleasure.) Use your hands to slightly flatten each portion. Bake on the top and center racks of the oven for 10 minutes (switching the baking sheets between top and center and rotating them 180 degrees halfway through the baking time) until slightly firm. Repeat with the remaining cookie dough, as necessary, once the baking sheets cool (hold the dough at room temperature). Remove from the oven, and cool the cookies on the baking sheets for 15 minutes.

ASSEMBLE THE SANDWICHES:

8. Remove the ice cream from the freezer. Line a baking sheet with parchment or wax paper. Place 10 cookies upside down on the baking sheet. Portion 5 level tablespoons or 1 level #12 ice-cream scoop of the ice cream onto each of the 10 cookies. Place another cookie, top side up, on the ice cream. Gently press the top cookies into place. Cover the sheet of sandwiches with plastic wrap and place in the freezer for several hours before decorating.

MAKE THE CHOCOLATE PEANUT BUTTER GANACHE AND DECORATE THE SANDWICHES:

9. Melt the chocolate with the peanut butter, heavy cream, and sugar in the top of a double boiler or in a medium glass bowl in a microwave oven (see Techniques, page 191) and stir until smooth.

10. Remove the ice cream sandwiches from the freezer. Let stand for a few minutes to slightly soften the ice cream (the ganache will not adhere to the ice cream if the sandwiches are rock hard).

continued

11. Place the peanuts in a medium bowl. Roll the ice cream edge of a sandwich in the ganache to cover all the ice cream, but not the cookie, with ganache. Then roll the ganache-coated sides in the peanuts to cover all the ganache with peanuts. Place the sandwich back on a baking sheet in the freezer, and repeat with the remaining sandwiches.

12. Once all the sandwiches have been decorated, wrap each individually with plastic wrap and place in a tightly sealed plastic container in the freezer until that happy time for festive consumption.

THE CHEF'S TOUCH

To make the melted peanut butter, place ¾ cup peanut butter in a 2-cup heatproof glass measuring cup and microwave for approximately 30 seconds (time will vary depending upon the wattage and power settings of your microwave oven).

If the Peanut Butter Ice Cream is too hard to scoop, soften it in the refrigerator for about 45 minutes.

These sandwiches will keep in the freezer for up to 2 weeks when individually wrapped in plastic wrap and stored in a tightly sealed plastic container.

If you like, you can spread the preparation over 2 days:

day 1: Make and freeze the Peanut Butter Ice Cream.

day 2: Make the Chocolate Drop Cookies. Once baked, cool the cookies at room temperature for at least 15 minutes before assembling. While the cookies are cooling, remove the ice cream from the freezer and place in the refrigerator. Make the Chocolate Peanut Butter Ganache. Assemble, decorate, and freeze the sandwiches as described.

chocolate golden rummy raisin ice milk

MAKES 1¼ QUARTS

Like a dark sky displaying the moons and the planets, this deep, dark chocolate ice milk is studded with a galaxy of rum-drenched golden raisins. Its unexpected richness will send you to celestial heights.

1 cup golden raisins

½ cup dark rum

6 ounces semisweet baking chocolate, coarsely chopped

2 ounces unsweetened chocolate, coarsely chopped

3½ cups whole milk

1 cup granulated sugar

3 large eggs

1. Place the raisins in a small bowl. Pour the rum over them and stir until coated. Cover the bowl with plastic wrap and set aside.

2. Melt the chocolates in ½ cup of the milk in the top of a double boiler or a medium glass bowl in a microwave oven (see Techniques, page 191) and stir until smooth.

3. Combine the remaining 3 cups milk and ½ cup of the sugar in a large saucepan over medium heat. Bring to a boil, stirring to dissolve the sugar.

4. While the milk is heating, place the remaining ½ cup sugar and the eggs in the bowl of a stand electric mixer fitted with a paddle. Beat on high for 2 to 3 minutes until thoroughly combined, then stop and scrape down the sides of the bowl. Beat on high for 2 minutes more, until slightly thickened and pale yellow.

5. If at this point the milk mixture has not started to boil, adjust the mixer speed to low and continue to mix until the milk does boil; otherwise, lumps may form when the milk is added. Gradually pour the boiling milk into the sugar and eggs and mix on low to combine, about 45 seconds. (To avoid splattering, use a pouring shield attachment or place a towel or plastic wrap over the mixer and down the sides to the bowl.)

6. Return the mixture to the saucepan, using a rubber spatula to scrape every dear drop from the bowl. Cook over medium heat, stirring constantly, until it reaches 185°F, 4 to 5 minutes. Use a digital thermometer (see Equipment, page 186) for an accurate reading.

7. Remove from the heat and strain through a fine-gauge strainer into a large stainless-steel bowl. Add the melted chocolate and stir to combine. Place the bowl in an ice-water bath to cool to 40° to 45°F. When the mixture is cold, freeze in an ice-cream machine following the manufacturer's instructions.

8. Transfer the ice milk to a 2-quart plastic container. Drain the raisins of any rum not absorbed. Add the raisins to the ice milk and stir with a rubber spatula to evenly distribute. Securely cover the container, and then place in the freezer for several hours before serving.

THE CHEF'S TOUCH

Yes, this thick, rich dessert is ice milk. Prepared with milk rather than the cream used in ice cream, the texture on your palate is lighter (and so are the calories). But the custard adds body and a velvety smooth texture not normally found in ice milk.

Some folks are sensitive to the sulfur dioxide that's used to keep the raisins made from Thompson seedless grapes golden. You can substitute regular raisins.

Chocolate Golden Rummy Raisin Ice Milk is at its best when served within 5 days of preparation. Keep the container securely covered in the freezer to prevent the ice milk from dehydrating and absorbing freezer odors.

been nice sweets

chocolate chip macadamia nut cookies

MAKES TWENTY-FOUR 3¼-INCH COOKIES

See photo, page 70

For me, it is impossible to reflect on Christmas and not immediately think of home-baked cookies. For many of us, chocolate chip cookies would dominate the musing. This chocolate chip cookie seeks a higher culinary standard with the addition of macadamia nuts. So smooth and buttery—these nuts almost steal the stage from the chocolate. Almost.

3 cups all-purpose flour

2 teaspoons baking powder

¼ teaspoon salt

1½ cups tightly packed dark brown sugar

8 ounces (2 sticks) unsalted butter, softened

2 large eggs

2 teaspoons pure vanilla extract

1½ cups whole raw unsalted macadamia nuts, toasted (see Techniques, page 192) and coarsely chopped

1½ cups semisweet chocolate chips

1. Preheat the oven to 300°F.

2. In a sifter, combine the flour, baking powder, and salt. Sift onto a large piece of parchment or wax paper.

3. Place the sugar and butter in the bowl of a stand electric mixer fitted with a paddle. Mix on low for 30 seconds, then on medium for 4 minutes. Stop and scrape down the sides of the bowl. Beat on high for 1 minute, then scrape down again. Beat on high for 1 minute more until the mixture is very soft. Add the eggs and vanilla, and beat on medium for 1 minute until combined. Scrape down again. Turn the mixer on to low and gradually add the dry ingredients; mix until incorporated, about 1 minute. Add the nuts and chocolate chips and mix on low for 30 seconds. Remove the bowl from the mixer, and use a rubber spatula to finish mixing the dough until thoroughly combined (this will take a bit of elbow grease as the dough is very dense).

4. Using 2 heaping tablespoons or 1 level #20 ice-cream scoop of the dough for each cookie, portion 6 cookies about 2 inches apart widthwise and lengthwise on each of 4 nonstick baking sheets. (If you don't have 4 sheets, use as many as you have and finish the rest once the sheets cool.) Place the baking sheets on the top and center racks of the oven and bake for 25 minutes, switching the sheets between top and center and rotating each sheet 180 degrees halfway through the baking time. (If you don't have room for all 4 sheets at one time, hold 2 at room temperature while the first 2 bake.) Remove from the oven and cool on the baking sheets for 5 minutes, then transfer the cookies to a cooling rack to cool to room temperature. Repeat with the remaining dough as necessary. Store the cooled cookies in a tightly sealed plastic container.

THE CHEF'S TOUCH

The association of macadamia nuts and Hawaii is so strong that not many would know that this unique nut is native to Australia. Cultivation of the tree for nuts did not start until the latter part of the nineteenth century, and not long after that the tree was exported to Hawaii where its success is borne out by the fact that Hawaii boasts some 90 percent of world production.

I suggest chopping macadamia nuts by hand with a cook's knife rather than in a food processor, which can render them macadamia nut butter (good on toast but not in this cookie).

The cookies will stay fresh in a tightly sealed plastic container at room temperature for 2 to 3 days or in the refrigerator for a week to 10 days (bring the cookies to room temperature before eating). The cookies may also be frozen in a tightly sealed plastic container for 5 to 6 weeks. Thaw the frozen cookies at room temperature before serving.

chocolate amaretto terrine

SERVES 10 TO 12

Granted that this dessert contains only a few ingredients—but oh my, this tempting list proves that short is sweet! I can't think of a slice of chocolate that delivers more pure "Joy to the World."

Vegetable pan spray

24 ounces semisweet baking chocolate, coarsely chopped

3⅓ cups heavy cream

2 cups sliced almonds, toasted (see Techniques, page 192) and coarsely chopped

2 ounces amaretto

GARNISH

Unsweetened whipped cream

1. Lightly spray a 9 × 5 × 2½-inch loaf pan with vegetable pan spray, then line the pan with plastic wrap.

2. Place the chocolate in a large heatproof bowl. Bring the cream to a boil in a medium saucepan over medium-high heat. Pour the cream over the chocolate and stir with a whisk until smooth.

3. Add the almonds and the amaretto, using a rubber spatula to fold them into the chocolate. Pour the mixture into the loaf pan. Cover the top of the terrine with plastic wrap and place in the freezer overnight.

4. Remove the terrine from the pan onto a clean, dry cutting board (if it does not slide out, pass an icing spatula or similar thin-bladed spatula around the inside edges between the plastic wrap and the pan). Remove and discard the plastic wrap. Heat the blade of a serrated knife under hot running water and wipe dry before cutting each slice. This slim terrine weighs in at a hefty 60 ounces, so you should be able to cut 10 to 12 slices. Accompany each slice with a cloud or two of unsweetened whipped cream. Let's hear another chorus of "Joy to the World."

THE CHEF'S TOUCH

You have to embrace a dessert that is so straightforward in ingredients and in preparation time and yet so glorious in taste. Yes, it must be frozen for several hours, but the wait will be rewarded by a dessert that will no doubt find space not only in your freezer but in your heart as well.

Amaretto, the apricot-almond liqueur, reinforces the almond presences in the terrine. Its absence, if you choose to eliminate it, would be regretful, but certainly not irredeemable. If amaretto is not to be found in your cupboard, a like amount of brandy would make a chummy substitution. But, after all, isn't it all about the chocolate?

This terrine may be prepared several days or even weeks before it is to be served. If you decide to keep it in the freezer for that period of time, keep the top of the terrine tightly wrapped with plastic wrap and cover the plastic wrap with aluminum foil. Not a bad idea to write the current date and the name of the dessert on the foil with a Sharpie®.

chocolate chunk celebrations

MAKES 18 CELEBRATIONS

These pocket-size chocolate beauties blend dessert categories: Are they cookies? Brownies? Cupcakes? All of the above? Whatever, they pack a punch of chocolate flavor, enhanced by chocolate chunks and the crunch of pecans. Celebrations celebrate Christmas or any other holiday.

18 ounces semisweet baking chocolate, coarsely chopped

8 tablespoons (1 stick) unsalted butter, cut into 1-tablespoon pieces

1 cup all-purpose flour

1 teaspoon baking powder

¼ teaspoon salt

¾ cup granulated sugar

4 large eggs

1 tablespoon pure vanilla extract

1 cup pecan halves, toasted (see Techniques, page 192) and coarsely chopped

4 ounces semisweet baking chocolate, chopped into ¼-inch chunks

1. Preheat the oven to 350°F. Place eighteen 2⅓-inch foil muffin cup liners on a baking sheet with sides.

2. Melt the coarsely chopped chocolate with the butter in the top of a double boiler or in a medium glass bowl in a microwave oven (see Techniques, page 191) and stir until smooth.

3. In a sifter, combine the flour, baking powder, and salt. Sift onto a large piece of parchment or wax paper.

4. Place the sugar and eggs in the bowl of a stand electric mixer fitted with a paddle. Beat on medium for 2 minutes until light in color and slightly thickened. Stop and scrape down the sides of the bowl, then add the melted chocolate and mix on low to combine, about 5 seconds. Gradually add the dry ingredients. Once all the dry ingredients have been incorporated, about 10 seconds, stop and scrape down again. Add the vanilla and mix on low for 5 seconds. Remove the bowl from the mixer, and use a rubber spatula to fold in the chopped pecans and the chocolate chunks and to finish mixing the batter until thoroughly combined.

continued

5. Portion 2 slightly heaping tablespoons or 1 level #20 ice-cream scoop of the batter into each foil liner. Place the baking sheet on the center rack in the oven and bake until a toothpick inserted in the center of a Celebration comes out almost clean but still slightly gooey, about 18 minutes. Rotate the baking sheet 180 degrees halfway through the baking time.

6. Remove the Celebrations from the oven and cool at room temperature for 30 minutes.

THE CHEF'S TOUCH

Former Trellis pastry chef Shelley Tennant and I developed the Chocolate Chunk Celebrations to celebrate the twenty-fifth anniversary of the Trellis Restaurant in Williamsburg, Virginia. Originally we thought the celebratory confection should be a cookie. As recipe testing ensued, we envisioned a cupcake-size item, but rather than the lightness of a traditional cupcake, we decided a texture between a cookie and a brownie would be perfect. So our Chocolate Chunk Celebrations now share space with our other celebrated cookies: Chocolate Black Gold Cookies, Mrs. D's Chocolate Chip Cookie, and Absolutely Deep Dark Chocolate Fudge Cookies in the cookie boxes we ship daily and in the big cookie jars at the Trellis bar (you wouldn't think we would sell pickled eggs at the Trellis bar!).

Keep the Celebrations in a tightly sealed plastic container, and they will stay fresh at room temperature for 4 to 5 days, or in the refrigerator for a week to 10 days (bring them to room temperature before eating). For maximum freshness when shipping, I suggest placing the Celebrations in tightly sealed resealable plastic bags before placing them in a shipping container.

chocolate almond cookie bark

MAKES SLIGHTLY MORE THAN 1¼ POUNDS

This magnificently simple yet highly addictive candy could leave chocolate lovers barking at the moon or, at least, at your back door howling for more.

6 Almond Cookies (see Santa's Workshop, page 166)

20 ounces semisweet baking chocolate, coarsely chopped

1. Line a baking sheet with sides with parchment or wax paper. Use your hands to break the Almond Cookies into approximately 1-inch pieces.

2. Melt the chocolate in the top of a double boiler or in a medium glass bowl in a microwave oven (see Techniques, page 191) and stir until smooth. Add the cookie pieces and use a rubber spatula to combine. Pour the mixture onto the baking sheet. Use a rubber spatula to spread the mixture as evenly as possible to the inside edges of the baking sheet.

3. Cover the baking sheet with plastic wrap and refrigerate until the bark is hard, about 30 minutes. To speed the process, you may place the bark in the freezer.

4. Remove the bark from the refrigerator or freezer and transfer to a cutting board. Use a cook's knife to cut the bark into pieces the size you want. Refrigerate in a tightly sealed plastic container.

THE CHEF'S TOUCH

A bunch of chocolate with almond cookies thrown in to give some interesting texture—simple but delicious. Feeling lazy? Substitute 1 cup toasted sliced almonds in place of the cookies—simpler and still tasty!

The only caveat about this candy is that the chocolate has not been tempered (a process that stabilizes the chocolate; think candy bars), and it will get messy if eaten out of hand. For that reason I recommend this as an adult treat or as an addition to a bowl of ice cream. Likewise, I do not recommend shipping the bark, but it easily takes a ride across town. (If you plan on taking the bark for a ride, separate the pieces with parchment or wax paper.)

Storing the bark in the freezer slows the melting time, and it is still quite delicious; plus, it will keep for several weeks. For those of us who like the pleasure of chocolate melting at body temperature, store the bark in a tightly sealed plastic container in the refrigerator for up to 5 days, or at room temperature, if not warmer than 74°F.

mocha meringue munches

MAKES 24 TO 28 MUNCHES

A bite of tantalizing perfection. These delicate baked cocoa meringues, bathed in a stimulating espresso glaze, create an expressive gift for your mouth that seems ever so momentary. You would be wise to bake a second batch to call your own.

COCOA MERINGUE

4 large egg whites

Pinch of cream of tartar

½ cup granulated sugar

1 tablespoon unsweetened cocoa powder

1 teaspoon cornstarch

ESPRESSO GLAZE

10 ounces semisweet baking chocolate, coarsely chopped

1 tablespoon instant espresso powder

MAKE THE COCOA MERINGUES:

1. Preheat the oven to 250°F. Line 2 baking sheets with parchment or wax paper.

2. Place the egg whites and the cream of tartar in the bowl of a stand electric mixer fitted with a balloon whip (the bowl and the whip need to be meticulously clean and dry; otherwise the egg whites will not whisk properly). Whisk on high for 2½ minutes until stiff peaks form. Add the sugar, cocoa, and the cornstarch and whisk on high until combined, about 5 seconds. Remove the bowl from the mixer, and use a rubber spatula to fold the meringue quickly but gently until all of the cocoa has been incorporated.

3. Fill a pastry bag with no tip with the meringue. Anchor the parchment onto the baking sheets with a tiny dab of meringue under each corner (this will keep the parchment from fluttering up during baking). Pipe 12 to 14 mounds of meringue on each of the baking sheets, each approximately 1½ inches high and 1¾ inches in diameter, about 1½ inches apart widthwise and lengthwise. Place the baking sheets on the top and center racks of the oven and bake for 1½ hours, until completely dry. Do not open the oven during the baking time; if you do, the oven temperature may drop and the meringues will not dry properly. Remove from the oven, and cool at room temperature for 20 minutes before removing from the paper.

MAKE THE ESPRESSO GLAZE AND GLAZE THE MUNCHES:

4. Melt the chocolate with the espresso powder in a double boiler or in a medium glass bowl in a microwave oven (see Techniques, page 191) and stir until smooth.

5. Remove the meringues from the paper. Handle the meringues gently and carefully as they are extremely brittle (a small offset spatula works effectively to loosen the meringues). Replace the used paper on the baking sheets with new.

6. One by one, hold a meringue by the base, dip the top about 1 inch into the melted chocolate, and gently shake off any excess chocolate. Place the chocolate-dipped meringue on its unchocolated bottom on the baking sheet. Repeat this procedure with the remaining meringues. If your kitchen is cool (70°F or less), the chocolate will set in 25 to 30 minutes. Otherwise, refrigerate the meringues for 10 to 15 minutes to allow the chocolate to set.

7. The Mocha Meringue Munches may be stored in a tightly sealed plastic container in a cool, dry place for up to 1 week.

THE CHEF'S TOUCH

Munches are perfect as a sophisticated sweet for your holiday celebration or any time a bite-size confection is the order of the day. Seems like that day is here!

Look for instant espresso powder at your local supermarket in the same general location as you would find instant coffee (if espresso powder is unavailable, you may substitute an equal amount of instant coffee).

A stand electric mixer fitted with a balloon whip makes short work of meringue preparation. The same whisking results, albeit not as pleasantly fast, can be achieved by hand or by using a handheld mixer.

A friendly reminder again: be nimble of finger when you handle the baked meringues, as they are delicate and break very easily.

ebony and ivory cookies

MAKES THIRTY-SIX 3-INCH COOKIES

All dressed up with nowhere to go? Not a chance with these elegant cookies. Ebony and Ivory Cookies bedeck your dining table and adorn your mouth with a confluence of white and dark chocolate—deck the halls with lots of cookies, fa la la la la, la la la la!

EBONY COOKIE

2 cups all-purpose flour

½ cup unsweetened cocoa powder

½ teaspoon salt

1 cup granulated sugar

4 tablespoons (½ stick) unsalted butter, cut into 1-tablespoon pieces

1 large egg

1 teaspoon pure vanilla extract

½ cup warm water (100° to 110°F)

1 teaspoon baking soda

½ cup buttermilk

2 cups semisweet chocolate mini morsels

EBONY ICING

4 ounces semisweet baking chocolate, coarsely chopped

4 ounces unsweetened baking chocolate, coarsely chopped

1 cup heavy cream

4 tablespoons granulated sugar

IVORY ICING

11 ounces white chocolate, coarsely chopped

1 cup heavy cream

MAKE THE EBONY COOKIES:

1. Preheat the oven to 350°F. Line 6 baking sheets with parchment or wax paper. (If you don't have that many, use as many as you have and hold the batter at room temperature until you can reuse some.)

2. In a sifter, combine the flour, cocoa, and salt. Sift onto a large piece of parchment or wax paper and set aside until needed.

3. Place the sugar and the butter in the bowl of a stand electric mixer fitted with a paddle. Beat on medium for 3 minutes until soft. Stop and scrape down the sides of the bowl and the paddle, then continue to beat on medium for 2 more minutes until very soft (at this point the mixture looks like wet sand). Scrape down again. Add the egg and the 1 teaspoon vanilla, and beat on medium for 30 seconds until combined. Scrape down again.

4. In a small bowl whisk together the warm water and the baking soda.

5. Turn the mixer on to low and gradually add the dry ingredients, then the buttermilk, then the water-soda mixture, and mix for 15 to 20 seconds. Stop and scrape down the sides of the bowl. Mix on medium for 30 seconds, until completely combined (don't be concerned that the mixture is lumpy). Remove the bowl from the mixer. Add the chocolate mini morsels and use a rubber spatula to finish mixing the batter

continued

until thoroughly combined (the mixture really does look more like a cake batter than a cookie dough).

6. Using 1 heaping tablespoon of batter or 1 heaping #70 ice-cream scoop of the batter, portion 6 cookies about 3 inches apart widthwise and lengthwise, onto each of the prepared baking sheets.

7. Place the baking sheets on the top and center racks of the oven and bake for 10 minutes, until the tops no longer appear wet, switching the sheets between top and center and rotating each sheet 180 degrees halfway through the baking time. Remove from the oven and cool on the baking sheets for 30 minutes. Repeat with the remaining cookie batter, as necessary, once the baking sheets cool (hold the batter at room temperature).

MAKE THE EBONY ICING:

8. Place the semisweet and unsweetened chocolates in a medium heatproof bowl. Bring the cream and sugar to a boil in a small saucepan over medium-high heat, stirring to dissolve the sugar. Pour the cream over the chocolate and stir with a whisk until smooth. Set aside at room temperature.

MAKE THE IVORY ICING:

9. Place the white chocolate in a medium heatproof bowl. Bring the cream to a boil in a small saucepan over medium-high heat. Pour the cream over the chocolate, and stir with a whisk until smooth. Refrigerate the Ivory Icing for 15 minutes before icing the cookies.

ICE THE COOKIES:

10. Turn the cookies over. Spoon approximately 1 heaping tablespoon of Ebony Icing onto half of the surface of each cookie. Spoon approximately 1 slightly heaping tablespoon of Ivory Icing over the other half of each cookie. Serve immediately (who could wait?).

THE CHEF'S TOUCH

Inspired by the black and white cookie made famous by Jerry Seinfeld, our version has the style that makes it perfect for holiday celebrations. Make these cookies and you'll gain the fame of Seinfeld—at least to those who get to eat them.

Ebony and Ivory Cookies will keep for several days stored at room temperature in a tightly sealed plastic container.

If you plan to produce the cookie for a gang and you want to get ahead of the game, the baked and cooled cookies (minus the icing) may be frozen for up to several weeks. Freeze in a tightly sealed plastic container to prevent the cookies from dehydrating and absorbing freezer odors. To serve, thaw the cookies, then ice as described.

coconut chocolate chunk macaroons

MAKES EIGHTEEN 3-INCH MACAROONS

In a traditional macaroon, almonds provide the dominant flavor. But this is the season to make merry, so let's throw restraint out the window and partner the almonds with sweet coconut and scrumptious chocolate chunks.

2 tablespoons unsalted butter, melted

1⅓ cups all-purpose flour

½ teaspoon baking soda

⅛ teaspoon salt

1 cup sliced almonds, toasted (see Techniques, page 192)

½ cup granulated sugar

½ cup tightly packed light brown sugar

4 large egg whites

⅛ teaspoon cream of tartar

6 ounces semisweet baking chocolate, chopped into ¼-inch pieces

1 cup sweetened flaked coconut

1. Preheat the oven to 350°F. Lightly coat 2 baking sheets with some of the melted butter. Line the sheets with parchment or wax paper, then lightly coat the paper with more melted butter.

2. In a sifter, combine the flour, baking soda, and salt. Sift onto a large piece of parchment or wax paper.

3. Place the almonds and the sugars in the bowl of a food processor fitted with a metal blade. Pulse for 10 to 12 seconds until combined and the almonds are coarsely chopped.

4. Place the egg whites and the cream of tartar in the bowl of a stand electric mixer fitted with a balloon whip (the bowl and the whip need to be meticulously clean and dry; otherwise the egg whites will not whisk properly). Whisk on high until stiff peaks form, about 2½ minutes. Remove the bowl from the mixer and use a rubber spatula to fold in half the almond mixture. When combined, fold in the remaining almond mixture. Fold in half of the sifted dry ingredients; when combined, fold in the rest. Now fold in half the chocolate and coconut, and when incorporated, fold in the rest until thoroughly combined.

continued

5. Using 2 slightly heaping tablespoon or 1 heaping #50 ice-cream scoop of the dough to portion 9 macaroons, about 2 inches apart widthwise and 3 inches apart lengthwise, on each of the baking sheets. Place the baking sheets on the top and center racks of the oven and bake for 15 to 16 minutes, until light golden brown, switching the sheets between top and center and rotating each sheet 180 degrees halfway through the baking time. Remove from the oven, and immediately transfer from the paper to a cooling rack to cool to room temperature (if the macaroons are not removed from the baking sheets within moments, they will stick to the paper). Store the cooled macaroons in a tightly sealed plastic container.

THE CHEF'S TOUCH

I experienced my first macaroon as a student at the Culinary Institute of America in the bake shop class, where they were on the agenda around the holidays. Made in the classic manner with almond paste, these cookies were a revelation to me. The first bite of slightly crunchy outer crust gave way to a soft but chewy center of remarkable flavor. Although I was immediately fond of the cookie, I found the almond paste to be a bit much. Today I prefer to use the nuts themselves to provide the almond flavor, and coconut to provide sweetness, and, as you would expect, chocolate plays a featured role in the mélange.

The macaroons will stay fresh in a tightly sealed plastic container at room temperature for 2 to 3 days, or in the refrigerator for a week to 10 days (to optimize the eating experience, bring the macaroons to room temperature first). For long-term storage (up to several weeks), freeze the macaroons in a tightly sealed plastic container to prevent them from dehydrating and absorbing freezer odors. Thaw the macaroons at room temperature before serving.

million dollar cookies

MAKES ABOUT EIGHTEEN 4-INCH COOKIES

These sweet, delectable cookies are worth their weight in gold: just the right amount of both white and dark chocolate, plus an abundance of pecans.

3 ounces white chocolate, coarsely chopped

2 cups all-purpose flour

1 teaspoon baking soda

½ teaspoon salt

1 cup tightly packed light brown sugar

½ cup granulated sugar

12 tablespoons (1½ sticks) unsalted butter, cut into 1-tablespoon pieces

2 large eggs

1 large egg yolk

2 cups pecan halves, toasted (see Techniques, page 192) and coarsely chopped (imagine a pecan half broken into 4 pieces)

10 ounces semisweet baking chocolate, chopped into ¼-inch pieces

1 teaspoon pure vanilla extract

1. Preheat the oven to 350°F. Line 3 baking sheets with parchment or wax paper.

2. Melt the white chocolate in the top of a double boiler or in a small glass bowl in a microwave oven (see Techniques, page 191), and stir until smooth.

3. In a sifter, combine the flour, baking soda , and salt. Sift onto a large piece of parchment or wax paper.

4. Place the sugars and butter in the bowl of a stand electric mixer fitted with a paddle. Mix on low for 1½ minutes, then beat on medium for 3 minutes until thoroughly combined. Stop and scrape down the sides of the bowl. Beat on medium-high for 2 minutes more until very smooth. Scrape down again. (Sad to say, the mixture looks like putty at this stage of the mixing. But the outcome is so delicious, it's worth a lack of aesthetics at this point.) Add the eggs and the egg yolk, one at a time, beating on medium for 30 seconds after each addition and scraping down the sides of the bowl once the eggs and yolk have been incorporated.

5. Add the melted white chocolate and beat on medium for 30 seconds until incorporated. Turn the mixer on to low and gradually add the dry ingredients; mix until incorporated, about 1 minute. Add the pecans, semisweet chocolate, and vanilla; mix until incorporated, about 30 seconds. Remove the bowl from the mixer, and use a rubber spatula to finish mixing the ingredients until thoroughly combined.

continued

6. Using 3 slightly heaping tablespoons or 1 slightly heaping #20 ice-cream scoop, portion 6 cookies about 2 inches apart widthwise and lengthwise on each baking sheet. Place the baking sheets on the top and center racks of the oven and bake for 18 to 19 minutes, switching the sheets between top and center and rotating each sheet 180 degrees halfway through the baking time. Remove the cookies from the oven and cool to room temperature on the baking sheets, about 30 minutes. Repeat with the remaining cookie dough, as necessary, once the baking sheets cool (hold the dough at room temperature). Store the cooled cookies in a tightly sealed plastic container.

THE CHEF'S TOUCH

Don't have a million dollars to give away at Christmas? This cookie is the next best thing.

At Ganache Hill, we have enough oven space to place two baking sheets parallel with each other on the same rack, so we can bake all 3 sheets of cookies at one time. If you are not able to do this in your oven, please don't be tempted to use the bottom rack of the oven—the cookies will burn! Simply wait for the first batch of 2 baking sheets to finish baking and then bake the third sheet of cookies (that has been held at room temperature).

Million Dollar Cookies will keep for several days at room temperature if stored in a tightly sealed plastic container. You can freeze the cookies for up to 3 to 4 weeks in a tightly sealed plastic container to prevent them from dehydrating and absorbing freezer odors.

chocolate mouthful of peanut butter bars

MAKES TWENTY-FOUR 2 × 2-INCH BARS

A tiny morsel of this peanut butter and chocolate confection will produce a paroxysm of pleasure, so imagine what a mouthful will do. It's okay to leave Santa some milk and store-bought pecan shortbreads, but save the Chocolate Mouthful of Peanut Butter Bars for the really special people in your life (and don't forget about me).

12 tablespoons (1½ sticks) unsalted butter, cut into 1-tablespoon pieces, plus 1 tablespoon, melted

1¼ cups plus 2 tablespoons all-purpose flour

4 ounces unsweetened baking chocolate, coarsely chopped

1 teaspoon salt

½ teaspoon baking soda

1 cup granulated sugar

4 large eggs

3 tablespoons dark corn syrup

½ cup buttermilk

1 teaspoon pure vanilla extract

1 cup peanuts, toasted (see Techniques, page 192)

1 cup creamy peanut butter, melted (see The Chef's Touch, page 90)

1. Preheat the oven to 325°F. Lightly coat a 13 × 9 × 2 inch nonstick baking pan with the melted 1 tablespoon butter. Flour the baking pan with 2 tablespoons of the flour; shake out any excess.

2. Melt the chocolate and the remaining 12 tablespoons butter in a double boiler or in a small glass bowl in a microwave oven (see Techniques, page 191) and stir until smooth.

3. In a sifter, combine the remaining flour, salt, and baking soda. Sift onto a large piece of parchment or wax paper.

4. Place the sugar, eggs, and corn syrup into a large bowl and stir with a whisk to combine. Add the melted chocolate and stir to combine. Add the dry ingredients and stir to combine. Add the buttermilk and the vanilla, and stir until incorporated. Finally, add the toasted peanuts, and use a rubber spatula to fold them into the batter.

5. Pour the batter into the prepared baking pan, spreading it evenly. Drizzle the peanut butter over the batter, and use a teaspoon to swirl it into the batter. Bake on the center rack of the oven until a toothpick inserted in the center comes out clean, about 35 minutes. (Rotate the pan 180 degrees halfway through the baking time.) Remove from the oven and cool in the pan at room temperature for 20 minutes.

continued

6. Use a serrated knife with a rounded tip to cut into twenty-four 2 × 2–inch bars. For a clean cut, heat the blade of the knife under hot running water and wipe dry before making each cut. Remove from pan and serve immediately or store in a tightly sealed plastic container at room temperature.

THE CHEF'S TOUCH

Melted peanut butter? The quickest way to accomplish this task is by measuring out the peanut butter into a 2-cup heatproof glass measuring cup and microwaving it for approximately 30 seconds (times will vary depending upon the wattage and power settings on your microwave oven).

The Chocolate Mouthful of Peanut Butter Bars will keep for 2 to 3 days stored in a tightly sealed plastic container at room temperature. For longer storage (4 to 5 days), cover the squares with plastic wrap or store in a tightly sealed plastic container in the refrigerator. Remove the brownies from the refrigerator 30 to 60 minutes before nibbling commences.

chocolate peppermint meringue cookies

MAKES 20 TO 22 COOKIES

This zingy cookie is a lightweight! Really just a mouthful of airy bliss highlighted by the cool crunch of peppermint candy and a tasty drizzle of chocolate. Let it snow meringue cookies!

¾ cup granulated sugar

2 teaspoons corn starch

3 large egg whites

1¼ teaspoons cream of tartar

24 individually wrapped red-and-white peppermint candies (about 4¾ ounces), coarsely chopped

3 ounces semisweet baking chocolate, melted (see Techniques, page 191)

1. Preheat the oven to 250°F. Line 2 baking sheets with parchment or wax paper.

2. In a small bowl combine the sugar and cornstarch.

3. Place the egg whites and the cream of tartar in the bowl of a stand electric mixer fitted with a balloon whip. Whisk on high for 2½ minutes until stiff peaks form. Add the sugar and cornstarch mixture; whisk on high until just incorporated, about 5 seconds. Remove the bowl from the mixer, add the peppermint candy, and use a rubber spatula to fold the meringue quickly but gently until all of the candy has been incorporated.

4. Fill a pastry bag with no tip with the meringue. Anchor the parchment onto the baking sheets with a tiny dab of meringue under each corner (this will keep the parchment from fluttering up during baking). Pipe 10 to 11 mounds of meringue on each of the baking sheets, each approximately 1 inch high and 2 inches in diameter, about 1 inch apart widthwise and 1½ inches apart lengthwise. Place the baking sheets on the top and center rack of the preheated oven and bake for 1½ hours until completely dry. Do not open the oven during the baking time; if you do, the oven temperature may drop and the meringues will not dry properly. Remove from the oven, and cool at room temperature for 20 minutes before removing the meringues from the paper.

5. Handle the meringues gently and carefully, as they are extremely brittle (I suggest you use a small offset spatula to loosen them from the paper, to prevent breakage). Replace the used paper on the baking sheets with new and place 10 to 11 meringues on each.

6. Use a teaspoon to drizzle thin lines of melted chocolate in a zigzag fashion over the tops of the meringues. If your kitchen is cool (70°F or less), the chocolate will set in 25 to 30 minutes; otherwise, refrigerate the meringues for 10 to 15 minutes to allow the chocolate to set.

continued

THE CHEF'S TOUCH

Although peppermint candies are widely popular year round, I am always reminded of my childhood Christmases in New England whenever I eat them. Never one to romance a hard candy by letting it melt in my mouth, I love the zing when I crunch the peppermint into dozens of tingly shards. With a second piece of candy, I feel transported to a simpler, less complicated era, when I didn't worry about book deadlines, mortgage payments, or trips to the dentist to repair cracked teeth. Our cookie may not turn back the calendar for you, but it will put that delightful zing in your mouth (and the hard candies will be precrunched!).

Chocolate Peppermint Meringue Cookies can be stored in a tightly sealed plastic container for up to 2 weeks at room temperature. Because of the delicacy of the meringue, I do not recommend longer-term storage of this cookie.

white chocolate banana spice mousse

SERVES 8

Sweet rewards to the dessert that enables the host to enjoy a stress-free preparation and presentation, and that is exactly what is offered in this simple but sophisticated holiday confection. A mousse ever so light, yet intriguing on the palate with the compelling flavor of banana and spices. Can't you just feel your mouth twinkling like the northern sky as Santa rides toward your table?

WHITE CHOCOLATE BANANA MOUSSE

2 cups heavy cream

2 tablespoons banana liqueur

10 ounces white chocolate, coarsely chopped and melted (see Techniques, page 191)

1 ripe medium banana (peeled and mashed)

WHIPPED CREAM

¾ cup heavy cream

2 teaspoons sugar

⅛ teaspoon pure vanilla extract

HOLIDAY SPICE BLEND

⅛ teaspoon ground cinnamon

⅛ teaspoon ground nutmeg

GARNISH

8 red or green maraschino cherries with stems

MAKE THE WHITE CHOCOLATE BANANA MOUSSE:

1. Place the cream into the bowl of a stand electric mixer fitted with a balloon whip. Whisk on high until stiff, about 2 minutes. Remove the bowl from the mixer. Use a rubber spatula to fold in the banana liqueur. Add about 1½ cups of this whipped cream to the melted white chocolate, and use a whisk to vigorously whisk together until thoroughly combined. Add this and the white chocolate back to the plain whipped cream; use a rubber spatula to fold together until smooth. Add the mashed banana, and use a rubber spatula to fold the mousse until well combined.

2. Refrigerate the mousse in a tightly sealed plastic container for 2 to 3 hours before serving.

MAKE THE WHIPPED CREAM:

3. Place the cream, sugar, and vanilla into the clean bowl of a stand electric mixer fitted with a balloon whip. Whisk on high until stiff peaks form, about 1 minute and 15 seconds. Remove the bowl from the mixer, and use a rubber spatula to scrape down the sides of the bowl and fold the cream until smooth and completely blended. Insert a star tip into a pastry bag and fill it with the Whipped Cream. Refrigerate until needed.

continued

MAKE THE HOLIDAY SPICE BLEND AND SERVE:

4. Sift the cinnamon and nutmeg through a small sifter into a small bowl.

5. Fill a pastry bag without a tip with the mousse. Pipe the mousse into eight 7-ounce champagne flutes to 1 inch of the top. Pipe the Whipped Cream onto the mousse. Sprinkle with the Holiday Spice Blend and top with a maraschino cherry. Refrigerate until just a few minutes before serving.

THE CHEF'S TOUCH

Mousse may be elemental to make, but it comes across as sophisticated rather than basic and is indeed very popular. The beauty with this dessert is that it may be prepared several hours or even the day before serving. Refrigerate the filled flutes until moments before serving.

Crowning each flute with a red or green maraschino cherry may seem retro, but it is also fun and colorful. If fun is in your nature, hold off the adornment until just before serving; otherwise, the cherry will discolor the whipped cream.

Another variation on this theme would be a pumpkin spice mousse: Use 1 cup canned pumpkin, ½ teaspoon ground nutmeg, and ½ teaspoon ground cinnamon in place of the mashed banana and banana liqueur.

If you only have one pastry bag, consider spooning the whipped cream onto the mousse rather than piping it.

chocolate peanut butter rocky road clusters

MAKES 14 CLUSTERS

Here is a toothsome candy that will get your favorite candy jockey on a sweet road of pleasure with every bite of chocolate, marshmallow, and nuts. The road may be rocky, but it sure is sublime.

16 ounces semisweet baking chocolate, coarsely chopped

3 tablespoons creamy peanut butter

1½ cups plain corn flakes (not frosted)

1½ cups miniature marshmallows

½ cup peanuts, toasted (see Techniques, page 192)

1. Line 2 baking sheets with parchment or wax paper.

2. Melt the chocolate and peanut butter in the top of a double boiler or in a medium glass bowl in a microwave oven (see Techniques, page 191), and stir until smooth.

3. Combine the corn flakes, marshmallows, and peanuts in a large bowl. Add the melted chocolate, and stir gently with a rubber spatula until all the ingredients are thoroughly combined.

4. Using 2 heaping tablespoons or 1 #20 ice-cream scoop, portion 7 clusters, about 1 inch apart, widthwise and lengthwise, on each baking sheet. For a slightly flatter cluster, use the back of the tablespoon to gently press down on each cluster. Refrigerate the clusters until firm, about 30 minutes.

THE CHEF'S TOUCH

The clusters will keep sweetly divine at room temperature (76°F or less) for several days. It's best to store them in individual clear treat bags or wax paper sleeves (you can locate the bags and sleeves in the cake decorating department of your local craft store), or you can individually wrap each cluster in wax paper, and place them in a tightly sealed plastic container. If the temperature is rising, refrigerate to avoid a meltdown.

white chocolate kisses

MAKES TWENTY-FOUR 2½-INCH KISSES

This wisp of a cookie is like a tiny, sweet kiss. The philosophy is simple—quick to make and to bake means more time for enjoying (the cookie and the kiss).

8 ounces (2 sticks) unsalted butter, cut into 1-tablespoon pieces and softened

1 tablespoon granulated sugar

Pinch of salt

2 large eggs

6 ounces white chocolate, coarsely chopped and melted (see Techniques, page 191)

½ teaspoon pure vanilla extract

2 cups all-purpose flour

24 Hershey's Kisses®

1 tablespoon confectioners' sugar

1. Preheat the oven to 300°F. Line 2 baking sheets with parchment or wax paper.

2. Place the butter, granulated sugar, and salt in the bowl of a stand electric mixer fitted with a paddle. Mix on low for 1 minute, then on medium for 2 minutes. Stop and scrape down the sides of the bowl and the paddle. Beat on medium-high for 2 minutes, until the butter is very soft and smooth. Scrape down again.

3. Add 1 egg and beat on medium for 30 seconds, then scrape down again. Add the second egg and beat on medium for 30 seconds, then on medium-high for 1 minute (the mixture looks like scrambled eggs, but it will magically come together when the chocolate is added). Scrape down again.

4. Add the white chocolate and the vanilla, and beat on medium for 30 seconds until incorporated. Stop and scrape down the sides of the bowl and the paddle. Turn the mixer on to low and gradually add the flour; mix until incorporated, about 30 seconds. Remove the bowl from the mixer, and use a rubber spatula to finish mixing the dough until thoroughly combined.

continued

5. Using 1 heaping tablespoon or 1 level #50 ice-cream scoop, portion 12 kisses on each baking sheet, about 1½ inches apart widthwise and lengthwise. Place a Hershey's Kiss in the center of each portion, gently pressing it about one fourth of the way into the dough. Place the baking sheets on the top and center racks of the oven, and bake for 14 minutes until lightly golden brown along the edges, switching the sheets between top and center and rotating each sheet 180 degrees halfway through the baking.

6. Remove the Kisses from the oven and cool to room temperature on the baking sheets. Once the Kisses are cool, use a fine-gauge strainer or a sifter to dust them uniformly with a light flurry of confectioners' sugar.

THE CHEF'S TOUCH

You may have noticed the relatively small amount of sugar in this dough: just 1 tablespoon. But coupled with the sugar in the white chocolate and the Hershey's Kiss, it is just the right amount to deliver a subtle sweetness and melt-in-your-mouth texture.

Notice the baking time is just 14 minutes, so you should avoid distractions like playing mouth music with your sweetie, and keep a close eye on your cookies as they bake. The Kisses can be stored in a tightly sealed plastic container at room temperature for up to 2 weeks. The Kisses may also be frozen in a tightly sealed plastic container for up to 5 weeks.

If you are shipping the Kisses, omit the dusting of confectioners' sugar, place them in resealable plastic bags, and seal tightly. The Kisses will be as delicious when they arrive as when they exited your oven.

chocolate cashew diamonds

MAKES 16 DIAMONDS

Only your dentist will bandy with this candy—a mouthful of engaging caramel-flavored, cashew-enhanced chocolate happiness. Although you will have to invest some jaw time in this chewy confection, every pleasure-filled munch will seem like a gift.

CASHEW DOUGH

5 tablespoons cold unsalted butter, cut into ½-tablespoon pieces, plus 1 tablespoon, melted

1 cup all-purpose flour

⅔ cup confectioners' sugar

2 large egg yolks

½ cup unsalted cashews, toasted (see Techniques, page 192) and coarsely chopped

CASHEW FILLING

12 tablespoons (1½ sticks) unsalted butter, cut into 1-tablespoon pieces

2 cups tightly packed light brown sugar

¾ cup heavy cream

⅔ cup light corn syrup

4 ounces unsweetened baking chocolate, cut into ¼-ounce pieces

2 cups unsalted cashews, toasted (see Techniques, page 192) and coarsely chopped

2 cups semisweet chocolate chips

10 ounces semisweet baking chocolate, coarsely chopped

MAKE THE CASHEW DOUGH:

1. Preheat the oven to 325°F. Lightly coat a 13×9×2-inch nonstick baking pan with some of the melted 1 tablespoon butter, then generously coat the sides with more melted butter (this will allow for easy removal of the baked confection).

2. Place the flour and confectioners' sugar in the bowl of a stand electric mixer fitted with a paddle. Mix on low for 10 seconds to blend the ingredients.

3. Add the cold butter one piece at a time while mixing on low, until mealy in texture, about 2 minutes. Add the egg yolks and mix on low until the dough forms around the paddle, about 30 seconds. Add the cashews and mix on low for 30 seconds, until the nuts are incorporated.

4. Remove the dough from the mixer, and form it into a ball (this will finish incorporating the nuts into the dough). Place in the prepared baking pan. Use your hands to flatten the dough uniformly to cover the bottom of the baking pan. Bake on the center rack of the oven for 15 minutes, until very light golden brown around the edges. Remove from the oven and set aside, and leave the oven turned on.

continued

MAKE THE CASHEW FILLING:

5. Bring the butter, brown sugar, cream, and corn syrup to a boil in a large saucepan over medium-high heat, stirring to dissolve the brown sugar. Boil for 3 minutes, until thickened, stirring constantly with a whisk. Remove from the heat. Add the unsweetened chocolate and stir until the chocolate has melted. Use a rubber spatula to fold in the chopped cashews and chocolate chips. Pour the filling onto the baked dough. Use a rubber spatula to spread evenly. Bake on the center rack of the oven for 30 minutes, until the mixture is bubbling on the surface. (Rotate the pan 180 degrees halfway through the baking time.)

6. Remove from the oven—handle carefully as the cashew filling will be bubbling hot—and immediately sprinkle the semisweet chocolate over the surface. Place the pan back in the oven for 3 minutes. Remove the pan from the oven, and use a spatula to smooth the chocolate. Cool at room temperature for 20 minutes, then refrigerate for 1 hour, until firm, before cutting.

PRESENTATION:

7. Remove the pan from the refrigerator. Turn the pan over onto a clean, dry, cutting surface (you may need to lightly tap one long edge of the pan against the cutting surface to dislodge the contents), then turn the contents chocolate side up. Using a sharp serrated knife (heat the blade under hot running water and wipe dry before each use), cut away ¼ inch of the edge from the two narrower ends, then divide widthwise into 4 strips. Diagonally trim a ½-inch piece from each end of each strip, then cut the strip diagonally 3 times to form 4 uniformly sized diamonds from each strip. The diamonds may be served immediately (only to those with good chewing capabilities) or kept at room temperature for 30 minutes (this will yield a slightly less chewy diamond).

THE CHEF'S TOUCH

Although nut-enhanced chocolate candies are legion, you will want to add this recipe to the top of your list. With the appropriate balance of flavor and texture, Chocolate Cashew Diamonds are a candidate for conspicuous consumption.

Purchase unsalted cashews in the bulk food section at your supermarket. Like many other nuts, for the best quality, purchase whole cashews rather than cashew pieces.

Unless you are a habitué of the cashew plantations of Brazil, you probably have never seen cashews in the shell. Called an apple but resembling a pear, the shell of the sweet cashew nut contains a toxic oil similar to poison ivy's, which causes the skin to itch and swell.

The Diamonds may be stored in a tightly sealed plastic container in the refrigerator for several days. They are best when brought to room temperature before eating.

cocoa coconut pumpkin chocolate chip muffins

MAKES 21 MUFFINS

Muffins for breakfast anyone? Oh, yes, especially when they are Cocoa Coconut Pumpkin Chocolate Chip Muffins, lavishly topped with a Bittersweet Chocolate Cream Cheese Icing. After all, it's Christmas.

COCOA COCONUT PUMPKIN CHOCOLATE CHIP MUFFINS

1¾ cup all-purpose flour

½ cup unsweetened cocoa powder

2 teaspoons baking powder

1 teaspoon ground allspice

½ teaspoons baking soda

½ teaspoon salt

1⅓ cups granulated sugar

8 tablespoons (1 stick) unsalted butter, cut into 1-tablespoon pieces and softened

3 large eggs

⅔ cup solid-pack pumpkin

½ cup buttermilk

1 teaspoon pure vanilla extract

1 cup semisweet chocolate chips

1 cup sweetened shredded coconut

BITTERSWEET CHOCOLATE CREAM CHEESE ICING

8 ounces (2 sticks) unsalted butter, cut into 1-tablespoon pieces and softened

One 8-ounce package cream cheese, softened

1 cup confectioners' sugar, sifted

3 ounces unsweetened baking chocolate, melted (see Techniques, page 191)

MAKE THE COCOA COCONUT PUMPKIN CHOCOLATE CHIP MUFFINS:

1. Preheat the oven to 325°F. Line each of 21 muffin tin cups with 2½-inch foil or paper liners.

2. In a sifter, combine the flour, cocoa, baking powder, allspice, baking soda, and salt. Sift onto a large piece of parchment or wax paper.

3. Place the sugar and butter in the bowl of a stand electric mixer fitted with a paddle. Mix on low for 1 minute, then beat on medium for 2 minutes. Stop and scrape down the sides of the bowl and the paddle. Beat on medium-high for 1 minute, until very soft. Add the eggs one at a time, beating on medium for 30 seconds after each addition, and scraping down again once the eggs have been incorporated. Add the pumpkin, and mix on medium for 30 seconds. (Don't be disappointed by the slimy appearance of the batter; the addition of the dry ingredients will pull things together.) Scrape down again. Turn the mixer on to low and gradually add the dry ingredients; mix until incorporated, about 20 seconds.

continued

Scrape down again. On low, add the buttermilk and the vanilla in a slow, steady stream (to avoid splattering) and mix until combined, about 10 seconds. Remove the bowl from the mixer, and use a rubber spatula to fold in the chocolate chips and coconut and to finish mixing the ingredients until thoroughly combined.

4. Portion 3 slightly heaping tablespoons or 1 slightly heaping #20 ice-cream scoop of batter into each muffin cup. Bake the muffins on the top and center racks of the oven until a toothpick inserted in the center of one of the muffins comes out ever so slightly moist with batter, about 20 minutes. (Switch the tins between the top and center and rotate each tin 180 degrees halfway through the baking time.) Remove the muffins from the oven, and cool at room temperature in the tins for 15 minutes. Remove the muffins from the tins (but not from the liners). Refrigerate the muffins while preparing the icing.

MAKE THE BITTERSWEET CHOCOLATE CREAM CHEESE ICING:

5. Place the butter and cream cheese in the clean bowl of a stand electric mixer fitted with a clean paddle. Mix on low for 1 minute, then beat on medium for 2 minutes. Stop and scrape down the sides of the bowl and the paddle. Beat on medium-high for 1 minute, until smooth. Scrape down again. Add the confectioners' sugar, and mix on low for 15 seconds until incorporated. Stop and scrape down the sides of the bowl and the paddle, then beat on medium for 30 seconds, until smooth.

6. Add the chocolate and beat on medium for 30 seconds, until the icing is smooth and combined. Remove the bowl from the mixer, and use a rubber spatula to finish mixing the icing until thoroughly combined.

7. Spread 2 slightly heaping tablespoons or 1 slightly heaping #50 ice-cream scoop of the icing onto each muffin, using the back of a dessert spoon to spread the icing. Serve immediately. The muffins may also be refrigerated in a tightly sealed plastic container. Bring the refrigerated muffins to room temperature before serving.

THE CHEF'S TOUCH

Check the label of the canned pumpkin so that you do not purchase pumpkin pie filling rather than solid-pack pumpkin. Pumpkin pie filling is laced with spices, and although the recipe calls for spices, doubling up will overly intensify that holiday flavor.

Once cooled, the muffins may be stored in a tightly sealed plastic container in the refrigerator for several days. The muffins may also be frozen, without icing, for up to 3 weeks. To prevent the muffins from absorbing freezer odors, place them in a tightly sealed plastic container. Bring to room temperature before icing and serving.

chocolate strawberry hazelnut brownie bars

MAKES TWENTY-FOUR 2 × 2-INCH BARS

If this is not an "uptown," dressed-up brownie, then I must be in the wrong neighborhood. Actually, fresh strawberries and sweet hazelnuts baked in a chocolate batter, topped with a Chocolate Hazelnut Ganache, should put this brownie in the penthouse suite. If you want Santa to visit your neighborhood, I suggest that these brownies are the perfect invitation.

CHOCOLATE STRAWBERRY HAZELNUT BROWNIES

12 tablespoons (1½ sticks) unsalted butter, cut into 1-tablespoon pieces, plus 1 tablespoon, melted

1¼ cups plus 2 tablespoons all-purpose flour

4 ounces unsweetened baking chocolate, coarsely chopped

1 pint fresh strawberries

1 teaspoon salt

½ teaspoon baking soda

1 cup granulated sugar

4 large eggs

½ cup buttermilk

3 tablespoons light corn syrup

1 teaspoon pure vanilla extract

1 cup hazelnuts, skinned and toasted (see Techniques, page 192) and coarsely chopped

CHOCOLATE HAZELNUT GANACHE

10 ounces semisweet baking chocolate, coarsely chopped

¾ cup heavy cream

2 teaspoons Frangelico® (hazelnut-flavored liqueur)

GARNISH

Vivacious Vanilla Ice Cream (see Santa's Workshop, page 181)

MAKE THE CHOCOLATE STRAWBERRY HAZELNUT BROWNIES:

1. Preheat the oven to 325°F. Lightly coat a 13 × 9 × 2–inch nonstick baking pan with the melted 1 tablespoon butter. Sprinkle the pan with 2 tablespoons of the flour. Shake out the excess.

2. Melt the 12 tablespoons butter and the unsweetened chocolate in the top of a double boiler or in a medium glass bowl in a microwave oven (see Techniques, page 191) and stir until smooth.

3. Gently rinse the strawberries in a colander with lukewarm water. Shake the colander to remove excess water. Stem, then cut the berries into about 1-inch chunks. In a sifter, combine the remaining 1¼ cups flour, the salt, and baking soda. Sift onto a large piece of parchment or wax paper.

continued

4. Place the sugar, eggs, buttermilk, corn syrup, and vanilla into a large bowl and stir with a whisk to combine. Add the melted chocolate and stir with the whisk to incorporate. Add the dry ingredients, and stir with the whisk to thoroughly combine (the batter will not be completely smooth). Use a rubber spatula to fold half of the berry pieces and ½ cup of the hazelnuts into the batter (set aside the remaining berries and hazelnuts for decoration later). Pour the batter into the prepared baking pan, spreading evenly with a rubber spatula.

5. Bake on the center rack of the oven until a toothpick inserted in the center comes out clean, about 30 minutes. (Rotate the pan 180 degrees halfway through the baking time.) Remove from the oven and cool in the pan at room temperature for 15 minutes, then refrigerate for 30 minutes before decorating.

MAKE THE CHOCOLATE HAZELNUT GANACHE:

6. Weigh out and set aside 4 ounces of the semisweet chocolate for decoration. Place the remaining 6 ounces chocolate in a medium heatproof bowl. Bring the heavy cream to a boil in a small saucepan over medium-high heat. Pour the cream over the chocolate, and stir with a whisk until smooth. Add the Frangelico and use the whisk to stir gently to combine.

7. Remove the brownies from the refrigerator. Pour the ganache over the brownies, and use a rubber spatula to spread it evenly over the entire surface. Sprinkle the reserved chocolate over the ganache, then the reserved berries, and finally the remaining ½ cup hazelnuts. Refrigerate the brownies for 1 hour (to firm the ganache enough to cut).

8. While the brownies are still in the pan, use a serrated knife with a rounded tip to cut into twenty-four 2-inch bars. For a clean cut, heat the blade of the knife under hot running water and wipe dry before making each cut. Serve 1 or 2 bars immediately with a generous scoop of Vivacious Vanilla Ice Cream, or store the bars in a tightly sealed plastic container in the refrigerator.

THE CHEF'S TOUCH

Don't be intimidated by the list of ingredients needed for this brownie. Your first extraordinarily moist and mouthwatering bite will validate your organizational and baking efforts.

If you do not have a bottle of the hazelnut-flavored liqueur Frangelico, you may omit it from the recipe or substitute it with another compatible liqueur, like Godiva.

Chocolate Strawberry Hazelnut Brownie Bars will keep for 4 to 5 days in a tightly sealed plastic container in the refrigerator. Remove from the refrigerator about 30 minutes before serving. To me, they seem to taste best when they are slightly cool, but they are also quite enjoyable when cold directly from the refrigerator.

chocolate dipped pistachio cigars

MAKES 12 COOKIES

The no-smoking zone does not apply with our pistachio-studded, chocolate-dipped cigar. Rather, this dainty cookie makes a heavenly treat with a cup of tea after all the presents have been wrapped.

6 tablespoons light corn syrup

¼ cup confectioners' sugar

2 level tablespoons all-purpose flour

½ teaspoon pure vanilla extract

2 tablespoons unsalted butter, melted

¼ cup shelled and skinned pistachios, toasted (see Techniques, page 192) and coarsely chopped

8 ounces semisweet baking chocolate, coarsely chopped

1. Preheat the oven to 300°F.

2. Place the corn syrup, confectioners' sugar, flour, and vanilla in a medium bowl, and then pour in the melted butter. Use a rubber spatula to stir until smooth. Add the chopped pistachios and use the spatula to thoroughly combine the ingredients.

3. Using 1 heaping teaspoon of batter for each cookie, portion 4 cookies about 3½ inches apart widthwise and lengthwise on each of 3 nonstick baking sheets (no need for parchment or wax paper). Bake only one of the baking sheets at a time (keep the other 2 baking sheets at room temperature) on the center rack in the preheated oven for 12 to 13 minutes until uniformly light golden brown (rotate the baking sheet 180 degrees halfway through the baking time). Allow to cool for 1 minute on the baking sheet before handling.

4. Use a small offset spatula to lift one cookie from the baking sheet; flip the cookie so the pistachios are on the outside, and using your fingers, roll into a cigar shape. Place on a room-temperature baking sheet and repeat the rolling process with the 3 remaining cookies. If the cookies become too hard to roll, pop them back into the oven for a few seconds; that will soften them enough to be rolled. Repeat with the remaining sheets of cookies.

continued

5. Melt the chocolate in a double boiler or in a small glass bowl in a microwave oven (see Techniques, page 191). One at a time, carefully dip about half the length of each cigar into the chocolate. Let the excess chocolate drip back into the double boiler before placing the cigar onto a baking sheet lined with clean parchment paper. Once all the cigars have been dipped in chocolate, refrigerate for a few minutes to firm the chocolate before serving.

THE CHEF'S TOUCH

The recipe for this cookie is obviously simple, with very few ingredients, effortless preparation, and quick baking time. What will take patience and practice is rolling the baked cookies into cigars. That is why I suggest baking only one sheet of 4 cookies at a time—once the cookies exit the oven you will need to work quickly in order to roll them while they are still warm. They harden once they start to cool, making rolling impossible. But don't forget that you may put the too-hard cookies back in the oven for a few seconds to soften them and try again. The aphorism "practice makes perfect" applies with this confection.

Note that the cookies will appear paper-thin while baking—and that's the way it is!

The rolled cookies—without the chocolate—may be kept in a tightly sealed plastic container for several days. Place parchment or wax paper in between the layers. Dip the cookies in chocolate and refrigerate just prior to serving.

chocolate peanut butter cups

MAKES 10 CUPS

Peanut butter and chocolate are certainly not strangers in the confectionery scene. This Chocolate Peanut Butter Cup shares the flavors and textures of a popular commercial peanut butter cup, but its pedigree makes it a candidate for a dessert plate rather than a paper wrapper.

CHOCOLATE CUPS

Twelve 6-inch squares aluminum foil

8 ounces semisweet baking chocolate, melted (see Techniques, page 191)

PEANUT BUTTER MOUSSE

One 8-ounce package cream cheese, softened

1 cup creamy peanut butter

¼ cup granulated sugar

⅔ cup heavy cream

¼ teaspoon pure vanilla extract

½ cup semisweet chocolate mini morsels

MAKE THE CHOCOLATE CUPS:

1. Line twelve 2-ounce ramekins with the aluminum foil, pushing down to shape the foil to the ramekins. (Although the recipe is for 10 peanut butter cups, I recommend using 12 ramekins to insure against the possibility of a broken chocolate cup or two.)

2. Using 1 slightly heaping tablespoon or a level #70 ice-cream scoop, portion the melted chocolate into each ramekin, then use the back of a teaspoon to spread the chocolate over the insides to completely cover the foil. Refrigerate the ramekins until the chocolate is thoroughly hardened, 30 to 40 minutes.

MAKE THE PEANUT BUTTER MOUSSE:

3. Place the softened cream cheese, peanut butter, and sugar in the bowl of a stand electric mixer fitted with a paddle. Beat on medium for 1 minute until combined. Stop and scrape down the sides of the bowl and the paddle. Beat on medium-high until very soft, about 1 minute. Transfer to another bowl and set aside.

4. Place the heavy cream and vanilla in a clean mixer bowl and attach a balloon whip. Whisk on high until stiff peaks form, about 1½ minutes. Use a rubber spatula to fold the whipped cream into the peanut butter mixture until thoroughly incorporated, then fold in the chocolate mini morsels.

continued

ASSEMBLE THE CHOCOLATE PEANUT BUTTER CUPS:

5. Remove the ramekins from the refrigerator and the foil cups from the ramekins. Very carefully remove the foil from each chocolate cup. (This is where the 2 extra chocolate cups can come in handy.)

6. Transfer the peanut butter mousse to a pastry bag fitted with a large star tip. Pipe the mousse into each cup so it peaks about 1 inch above the top of the cup. Refrigerate for at least 30 minutes before serving.

THE CHEF'S TOUCH

Our pastry chef at the Trellis frequently features a trio of desserts as the pastry chef's selection, and this sweet little confection is often one of the stars of the plate.

You can do the same thing, using this book. My suggested trio includes a Chocolate Peanut Butter Cup, a Chocolate Cashew Diamond (page 103), and a 4-ounce ramekin of Chocolate Mint Bourbon Crème Brûlée (page 135). That's a triumvirate that would have no problem ruling.

If serving the Chocolate Peanut Butter Cups as the solo star, you may want to serve two cups per portion. Accompany the duo with Peanut Butter Berry Sauce (page 179), and you have a berry nice dessert.

To reinforce the presence of the mini morsels, sprinkle a few over the mousse in each chocolate cup.

You may store the Chocolate Peanut Butter Cups in a tightly sealed plastic container in the refrigerator for 2 to 3 days.

chocolate gingerbread snowflakes

MAKES 24 COOKIES

Chocolate and spice make nice with this ethereal snowflake cookie, as pleasing to the eye as to the tummy. Chocolate Gingerbread Snowflakes are certain to bring a smile and the sweet promise of the holiday season.

1¾ cups all-purpose flour

½ cup unsweetened cocoa powder

1 teaspoon baking powder

2 teaspoons ground ginger

1 teaspoon ground allspice

1 teaspoon salt

½ teaspoon ground cinnamon

¼ teaspoon ground cloves

8 tablespoons (1 stick) unsalted butter, cut into 1-tablespoon pieces and softened

⅓ cup tightly packed dark brown sugar

2 tablespoons mild molasses

3 large egg yolks

¼ cup confectioners' sugar

1. Preheat the oven to 325°F. Line 3 baking sheets with parchment or wax paper.

2. In a sifter, combine 1½ cups of the flour, the cocoa, baking powder, ginger, allspice, salt, cinnamon, and cloves. Sift onto a large piece of parchment or wax paper.

3. Place the butter, brown sugar, and molasses in the bowl of a stand electric mixer fitted with a paddle. Mix on low for 1 minute, then on medium for 1½ minutes more. Stop and scrape down the sides of the bowl and the paddle. Add the egg yolks one at a time, beating on medium for 30 seconds after each addition, and scraping down again once all the yolks have been incorporated. Turn the mixer on to low and gradually add the dry ingredients; mix until a dense dough is formed, about 30 seconds. Remove the bowl from the mixer.

4. Using some of the remaining ¼ cup flour as needed, lightly flour a clean, dry work surface. Transfer the dough to the work surface and knead gently to form a smooth ball. Roll out the dough to ¼ inch thick (adding flour as necessary to prevent sticking). Cut the dough into about 15 snowflakes using a 3-inch snowflake cookie cutter. Form the remaining dough into a ball, roll out again, and cut about 6 snowflakes. Again form the remaining dough into a ball, roll out, and cut about 3 snowflakes. (At this point, any remaining dough has probably absorbed too much flour and should be discarded.) Place 8 snowflakes, evenly spaced about 2 inches apart widthwise and 2 inches apart lengthwise, onto each of the baking sheets.

5. Bake on the top and center racks in the oven for 8 to 9 minutes, or for 6 to 7 minutes if you prefer a softer cookie, switching the sheets between top and center and rotating each sheet 180 degrees halfway through the baking time. Remove from the oven, and cool on the baking sheets at room temperature. Once the snowflakes are cool, let it snow by sifting the confectioners' sugar liberally over the cookies. Store the snowflakes in a tightly sealed plastic container.

THE CHEF'S TOUCH

We purchased our snowflake cookie cutter at our local Wal-Mart. Many other cookie cutters may be used with this cookie dough, including the ever-popular gingerbread man. Whatever the choice, the delightful flavor of this cocoa and spice combination is certain to make kids of all ages happy.

The subtle, mild molasses we use at Ganache Hill is Grandma's® Unsulphured Original Molasses.

Chocolate Gingerbread Snowflakes will stay fresh in a tightly sealed plastic container at room temperature for 2 to 3 days or in the refrigerator for a week (bring the snowflakes to room temperature before eating). For longer storage (up to several weeks), freeze the cookies—before adding the confectioners' sugar—in a tightly sealed plastic container. Thaw the frozen cookies at room temperature, and then let it snow confectioners' sugar before serving.

cup o' dark chocolate

MAKES 8 CUPS

Chocolate no doubt is your cup of tea. One Cup o' Dark Chocolate may forever change the way you view what the contents of a cup should be. Warm dark chocolate ganache, chilled whipped cream, a spoon, and you—that's all that's needed for a state of ecstasy.

3¼ cups heavy cream

12 ounces high-quality semisweet chocolate, coarsely chopped

4 ounces high-quality unsweetened baking chocolate, coarsely chopped

2 tablespoons granulated sugar

GARNISH

Pistachio Raisin Biscotti (see Santa's Workshop, page 172), optional

1. Place ¾ cup of the heavy cream in the bowl of a stand electric mixer fitted with a balloon whip. Whisk on high until stiff, about 1 minute (this should yield 1½ cups of whipped cream). Refrigerate the whipped cream until needed.

2. Place the chocolates in a large heatproof bowl. Bring the remaining 2½ cups heavy cream and the sugar to a boil in a medium saucepan over medium heat, stirring to dissolve the sugar. Pour the cream over the chocolate and stir with a whisk until smooth.

3. Pour an equal amount of the chocolate ganache into 8 of your favorite coffee cups, filling each about halfway. Top each serving with a couple tablespoons of whipped cream. Enjoy while warm using a spoon or a cookie, such as our Pistachio Raisin Biscotti.

THE CHEF'S TOUCH

I suggest purchasing the best chocolate money can buy for this particular dessert, since not many ingredients in the recipe come between the chocolate and the chocolate lover. If you don't have a favorite gourmet chocolate, ask for suggestions at a specialty grocery store. The ideal semisweet chocolate for this recipe is dark, smooth, and delicious directly from the wrapper. For the unsweetened, find the best baking chocolate available, preferably with a high percentage of cocoa solids.

Tempered glass cups with a pedestal base, typical of those used for Irish coffee and other hot drinks, are perfect for a Cup o' Dark Chocolate (seeing the chocolate through the glass is part of the sensual experience).

cranberry chocolate chip oatmeal cookies

MAKES EIGHTEEN 4-INCH COOKIES

What a merry berry is our native American cranberry. Crimson-colored cranberries galore stud this whopper of a cookie. Of course, there are also chocolate chips, and to keep you on the good side of Santa's list, the cookie includes healthful oats.

2 cups all-purpose flour

1 teaspoon baking soda

1 teaspoon ground cinnamon

1 teaspoon salt

8 ounces (2 sticks) unsalted butter, cut into 1-tablespoon pieces and softened

1 cup tightly packed light brown sugar

¾ cup granulated sugar

2 large eggs

2 teaspoons pure vanilla extract

2 cups semisweet chocolate chips

2 cups quick oats

1½ cups dried cranberries

1. Preheat the oven to 325°F. Line 3 baking sheets with parchment or wax paper.

2. In a sifter, combine the flour, baking soda, cinnamon, and salt. Sift onto a large piece of parchment or wax paper.

3. Place the butter, brown sugar, and granulated sugar in the bowl of a stand electric mixer fitted with a paddle. Mix on low for 1 minute, then beat on medium for 2 minutes until thoroughly combined. Stop and scrape down the sides of the bowl and the paddle. Beat on medium-high for 2 minutes more, until very smooth. Scrape down again. Add the eggs one at a time, beating on medium for 30 seconds after each addition and scraping down again once the eggs have been incorporated. Add the vanilla and beat on medium for 15 seconds. Turn the mixer to low and gradually add the dry ingredients; mix until incorporated, about 1 minute. Add the chocolate chips, oats, and cranberries and mix on low until incorporated, about 30 seconds.

4. Remove the bowl from the mixer; and use a rubber spatula to finish mixing the ingredients until thoroughly combined (it may be easier to forgo the spatula and use your hands—you decide).

continued

5. Using 3 heaping tablespoons or 1 heaping #20 ice-cream scoop of dough for each cookie, portion 6 cookies onto each baking sheet, about 3 inches apart widthwise and lengthwise. Bake on the top and center racks of the oven for 15 minutes, switching the sheets between top and center and rotating each sheet 180 degrees halfway through the baking time. If you have limited oven space or baking sheets, keep the dough at room temperature while baking whatever number of cookies you can. Remove from the oven and cool to room temperature on the baking sheets, about 30 minutes. Store in a tightly sealed plastic container.

THE CHEF'S TOUCH

Everyone knows that oats are wholesome, but they also lend texture and moisture to cookies. Although I consume oats every morning at breakfast to reduce my cholesterol levels, I occasionally enjoy one or two of these cookies because they are just so darn good.

Cranberry Chocolate Chip Oatmeal Cookies will keep for several days at room temperature in a tightly sealed plastic container and for 2 to 3 weeks when stored in the refrigerator in a tightly sealed plastic container. If you are planning ahead for a holiday bash, you can freeze the cookies for several weeks in a tightly sealed plastic container to prevent them from dehydrating and absorbing freezer odors.

cocoa coconut cuties

MAKES SIXTEEN 2½-INCH COOKIES

Your cutie is gonna love you if he or she finds a box of Cocoa Coconut Cuties under the tree. These cookies are the perfect partnership of cocoa and coconut so they are not too sweet, but that special someone will think you are sweet for baking a batch.

1 cup confectioners' sugar

¾ cup all-purpose flour

¼ cup unsweetened cocoa powder

½ teaspoon baking powder

8 tablespoons (1 stick) unsalted butter, cut into 1-tablespoon pieces and softened

3 large egg whites

1¼ cups sweetened shredded coconut

1. Preheat the oven to 300°F. Line 2 baking sheets with parchment or wax paper.

2. In a sifter, combine the confectioners' sugar, flour, cocoa, and baking powder. Sift onto a large piece of parchment or wax paper.

3. Place the butter in the bowl of a stand electric mixer fitted with a paddle. Mix on low for 1 minute, then on medium for 1 minute, then on high for 1 minute. Stop and scrape down the sides of the bowl and the paddle. Add the egg whites and beat on medium for 30 seconds (at this point the nascent cookie dough looks temporarily yucky). Turn the mixer to low and gradually add the sifted ingredients; mix until incorporated, about 1 minute. Stop and scrape down the sides of the bowl and the paddle, and mix on low for an additional 5 seconds. Remove the bowl from the mixer. Add 1 cup of the shredded coconut, and use a rubber spatula to finish mixing the dough until thoroughly combined (now the dough is looking good).

4. Using 1 heaping tablespoon or 1 level #50 ice-cream scoop of dough, portion 8 cookies on each of the baking sheets about 3 inches apart widthwise and 2 inches apart lengthwise. Sprinkle an equal amount (about ¼ teaspoon) of the remaining coconut onto each portion. Bake on the top and center racks of a preheated oven for 12 minutes, switching the sheets between top and center and rotating each sheet 180 degrees halfway through the baking time. Remove from the oven and cool at room temperature on the baking sheets. Store the cooled cookies in a tightly sealed plastic container.

THE CHEF'S TOUCH

For an even cuter Cutie, I suggest the following: Melt 8 ounces coarsely chopped semisweet baking chocolate in a double boiler or in a small glass bowl in a microwave oven (see Techniques, page 191). Once the cookies have cooled to room temperature, dip the top of each cookie into the melted chocolate. Let the excess chocolate drip back into the double boiler before placing, chocolate side up, onto a baking sheet lined with parchment paper. Sprinkle ¼ teaspoon coconut onto each cookie. Refrigerate for a few minutes to firm the chocolate before serving.

Cocoa Coconut Cuties will stay fresh in a tightly sealed plastic container at room temperature for 2 to 3 days or in the refrigerator for up to 10 days (bring to room temperature before eating). Undipped, unsprinkled cookies may be frozen in a tightly sealed plastic container for several weeks. Thaw the frozen cookies at room temperature before serving.

been naughty sweets

chocolaty fudge cake

SERVES 10 TO 12

See photo, page 126

Granted, it's a little old-fashioned: two moist layers of fudge cake covered not just with chocolate icing but with honest-to-goodness fudge icing. Just the way Mom makes it.

HEAVY FUDGE ICING

2 cups tightly packed dark brown sugar

2 cups heavy cream

8 ounces semisweet baking chocolate, broken into ½-ounce pieces

6 tablespoons (¾ stick) unsalted butter, cut into 1-tablespoon pieces

CHOCOLATY FUDGE CAKE

8 ounces (2 sticks) unsalted butter, cut into 1-tablespoon pieces, plus 2 teaspoons, melted

1¾ cups all-purpose flour

½ teaspoon baking soda

¼ teaspoon salt

8 ounces semisweet baking chocolate, coarsely chopped

1¼ cups granulated sugar

3 large eggs

½ cup buttermilk

1 teaspoon pure vanilla extract

MAKE THE HEAVY FUDGE ICING:

1. Bring the brown sugar, cream, chocolate, and butter to a boil in a medium saucepan over medium-high heat, stirring to dissolve the sugar and melt the chocolate and butter. Adjust the heat to medium-low and simmer for 25 minutes, stirring frequently, until thickened and smooth. Remove from the heat. Pour into a baking sheet with sides and use a rubber spatula to spread evenly. Refrigerate for 2 hours, until chilled thoroughly.

MAKE THE CHOCOLATY FUDGE CAKE:

2. Preheat the oven to 325°F. Lightly coat two 9 × 1½–inch cake pans with some of the melted 2 teaspoons butter. Line the bottom of the pans with parchment or wax paper, then lightly coat the paper with more melted butter.

3. In a sifter, combine the flour, baking soda, and salt. Sift onto a large piece of parchment or wax paper.

4. Melt the chocolate and the remaining 8 ounces butter in the top of a double boiler or in a medium glass bowl in a microwave oven (see Techniques, page 191); stir until smooth.

5. Place the granulated sugar and eggs in the bowl of a stand electric mixer fitted with a paddle. Beat on medium-high for 2 minutes, until slightly thickened and pale yellow in color. Add the melted chocolate and mix on low to combine, about 15 seconds. Turn the mixer to low and gradually add the dry ingredients; mix until incorporated, about 30 seconds. Stop and scrape down the sides of the bowl. Add the buttermilk and vanilla and mix on low to combine, about 15 seconds. Remove the bowl from the mixer, and use a rubber spatula to finish mixing the batter until thoroughly combined.

6. Immediately divide the batter into the prepared pans, spreading evenly with a rubber spatula. Bake on the center rack of the oven until a toothpick inserted into the center of each layer comes out clean, 28 to 30 minutes. Remove from the oven and cool in the pans at room temperature for 15 minutes. Invert the cake layers onto cake circles or cake plates. Carefully peel the paper away from the bottom of each layer. Refrigerate the cake layers, uncovered, for at least 2 hours before assembling.

7. Transfer the chilled fudge to the bowl of a stand electric mixer fitted with a paddle. Beat on high for 2 minutes until lighter in color (a very mellow chocolate brown) and slightly fluffy.

8. Remove the cake layers from the refrigerator. Use an icing spatula to evenly and smoothly spread 2½ cups of the icing over the top and sides of one of the inverted layers (baked top down). Place a second layer, baked top up, on the icing and gently press it into place. Evenly and smoothly spread the remaining icing onto the top and sides of the cake. Refrigerate the cake for 1 hour before slicing and serving.

9. Heat the blade of a serrated knife under hot running water and wipe dry before cutting each slice. Serve immediately.

THE CHEF'S TOUCH

I created this cake with my mom in mind. When I think of Mrs. D in the kitchen of our Rhode Island home, I can imagine her reaching for a red box of Baker's chocolate, with my five sisters and me waiting anxiously for whatever chocolate concoction she would conjure. The sensual delight of this chocolaty-smooth cake makes it perfect for a Christmas celebration, as a gift, or even for dessert tonight.

The assembled cake may be kept in the refrigerator for up to 3 days before serving. To prevent the cake from absorbing refrigerator odors, store it in a tightly sealed plastic container. This container is also the perfect vehicle for transporting the cake to a Christmas celebration somewhere beyond your own home.

white chocolate banana walnut christmas log

SERVES 12

This iconoclastic take on the traditional French Christmas cake, *bûche de Noël*, will wow your senses visually and gastronomically. Instead of the French standard of a sponge cake filled with chocolate-flavored whipped cream or mousse, our version has an ethereal banana cake doing rings around a textural chocolate walnut ganache. An extraordinary dark chocolate buttercream completes this horticultural illusion that looks (and is) good enough to eat.

CHOCOLATE WALNUT GANACHE

8 ounces semisweet baking chocolate, coarsely chopped

¾ cup heavy cream

¾ cup walnut halves, toasted (see Techniques, page 192) and coarsely chopped

WHITE CHOCOLATE BANANA MOUSSE CAKE

4 tablespoons (½ stick) unsalted butter, plus 1 tablespoon, melted

12 ounces white chocolate, coarsely chopped

10 large egg yolks

¾ cup granulated sugar

2 tablespoons banana liqueur

½ cup all-purpose flour, sifted

1 ripe medium banana, peeled and mashed

6 large egg whites

1 tablespoon confectioners' sugar

DARK CHOCOLATE BUTTERCREAM

12 tablespoons (1½ sticks) unsalted butter, cut into 1-tablespoon pieces and softened

4 ounces unsweetened baking chocolate, coarsely chopped and melted (see Techniques, page 191)

1 cup confectioners' sugar, sifted onto a large piece of parchment paper (or wax paper)

MAKE THE CHOCOLATE WALNUT GANACHE:

1. Place the semisweet chocolate in a medium heatproof bowl. Bring the cream to a boil in a small saucepan over medium heat. Pour the cream over the chocolate; stir with a whisk until smooth. Add the walnuts and stir with a rubber spatula to combine. Set aside at room temperature.

MAKE THE WHITE CHOCOLATE BANANA MOUSSE CAKE:

2. Preheat the oven to 325°F. Lightly coat a 17 ¼ × 11½ × 1–inch jelly roll pan with some of the melted 1 tablespoon butter. Line the bottom of the pan with parchment or wax paper; lightly coat the paper with more melted butter. Set aside.

3. Melt the chopped white chocolate and the remaining 4 tablespoons butter in the top half of a double boiler over low heat (see Techniques, page 191), stirring constantly with a rubber spatula until the chocolate and butter are completely melted and smooth (4 to 5 minutes; if the water begins to simmer, remove the double boiler from the heat and continue to stir). Remove from the heat.

4. Place the egg yolks, ½ cup of the granulated sugar, and the banana liqueur in the bowl of a stand electric mixer fitted with a paddle. Beat on high for 2 minutes. Use a rubber spatula to scrape down the sides of the bowl. Beat for 2 minutes more on high until the mixture is pale yellow and slightly thickened. Add the melted white chocolate mixture to the egg yolks and beat on medium-high until thoroughly incorporated, about 30 seconds. Remove the bowl from the mixer. Use a rubber spatula to fold the flour into the egg yolk mixture. Fold in the mashed banana until thoroughly incorporated. Transfer the mixture to a large bowl and set aside.

5. Place the egg whites in the clean bowl of a stand electric mixer fitted with a balloon whip (the bowl and the whip need to be meticulously clean and dry; otherwise the egg whites will not whisk properly). Whisk the egg whites on high for 45 seconds, until soft peaks form, then gradually add the remaining ¼ cup granulated sugar and continue to whisk on high until stiff peaks form, about 45 seconds. Remove the bowl from the mixer. Add about a third of the egg whites to the batter; using a rubber spatula, fold to incorporate. Add the remaining egg whites, and fold the mixture until uniform in color.

6. Pour the batter into the prepared jelly roll pan, spreading evenly to the edges with a rubber spatula. Bake on the center rack of the oven until a toothpick inserted in the center of the cake comes out clean, about 22 minutes. (Rotate the pan 180 degrees halfway through the baking time.)

ASSEMBLE THE LOG:

7. While the cake is baking, sprinkle an 18 × 12–inch piece of parchment or wax paper with the tablespoon of confectioners' sugar (this is to prevent the very sticky cake from adhering to the paper).

8. Remove the cake from the oven. If any edges of the cake have not pulled away from the sides of the pan, use a sharp, thin-bladed paring knife to carefully cut the cake away from the sides. Immediately invert the cake onto the sugar-sprinkled paper. Gently peel the paper away from the bottom of the cake and discard. Cool at room temperature for 15 minutes.

9. Spread the Chocolate Walnut Ganache in an even layer to within ½ inch of the edges of the cake. Begin rolling the log away from you, starting with the narrow end and using the paper to help lift the cake over onto itself. Continue to roll the cake to the opposite end, making a tight roll. Wrap the parchment around the log, then wrap with plastic wrap. Transfer the log to a baking sheet and place in the freezer for 3 hours before icing.

MAKE THE DARK CHOCOLATE BUTTERCREAM:

10. While the log is in the freezer, place the butter in the bowl of a stand electric mixer fitted with a paddle. Mix on low for 1 minute; then increase the speed to medium-high and beat for 2 minutes. Stop and scrape down the sides of the bowl and the paddle. Beat on medium-high for 2 minutes more until very soft. Scrape down again. Add the unsweetened chocolate and beat on medium for 30 seconds. Scrape down again. Gradually add the confectioners' sugar while mixing on the lowest speed until combined, about 15 seconds, then beat on medium-high for 30 seconds until very soft and slightly fluffy. Remove the bowl from the mixer, and use a rubber spatula to finish mixing the icing until thoroughly combined. Cover with plastic wrap and set aside at room temperature.

continued

ICE THE LOG AND SERVE:

11. Remove the log from the freezer. Unwrap the log and discard the plastic wrap and parchment paper. Carefully place the log, seam side down, on a clean cooling rack or baking sheet. Use an icing spatula to evenly spread the buttercream over the top and sides, but not the ends (and not the seam-side bottom), of the log. Refrigerate until ready to serve.

12. To serve, use a serrated knife to trim a ¼-inch-thick slice from each end of the log. Cut the log into twelve 1-inch-thick slices. Heat the blade of a serrated knife under hot running water and wipe dry before cutting each slice. Serve immediately.

THE CHEF'S TOUCH

A medium-size banana should weigh 5 to 5½ ounces unpeeled and yield about 4 ounces of peeled fruit. Avoid overripe bananas; choose fruit with yellow skin and few or no brown spots. If bananas are still green, ripen them at room temperature for 2 to 3 days (plan ahead).

After assembly, you may keep the log in the refrigerator for 2 to 3 days before serving. To prevent the log from absorbing refrigerator odors, store it in a tightly sealed plastic container.

chocolate mint bourbon crème brûlée

MAKES 6 CRÈMES BRÛLÉES

"Sensual self-indulgence" is a custard that goes by the name of crème brûlée (literal translation: burnt cream). Crème brûlée's chapeau of brittle caramelized sugar actually inspired the name of this beloved dessert. Our version—a chocolaty, velvety smooth, bourbon-spiked custard that bathes your mouth with pleasure—is a delightful respite from being good for Christmas.

3 cups heavy cream

1 vanilla bean, cut in half lengthwise

¼ teaspoon salt

¾ cup plus 2 tablespoons granulated sugar

6 large egg yolks

9 ounces semisweet baking chocolate, coarsely chopped

1 tablespoon bourbon

½ teaspoon peppermint extract

GARNISH (OPTIONAL)

Mint sprigs

MAKE THE CRÈME BRÛLÉE:

1. Preheat the oven to 300°F. Pour 2 cups water into a 13 × 9 × 2–inch baking pan. Place the pan on the center rack of the oven.

2. Combine the cream, vanilla bean, and salt in a medium saucepan over medium heat. Bring to a boil, then remove from the heat.

3. Place ¾ cup of the sugar and the egg yolks in a medium mixing bowl. Whisk until thoroughly combined. Ladle ½ cup of the hot cream into the yolks and whisk gently to incorporate. Pour the egg yolk and cream mixture back into the saucepan and whisk until thoroughly combined. Add the chopped chocolate, and stir gently to melt the chocolate and incorporate all of the ingredients.

4. Pour the chocolate custard through a fine-gauge strainer into a 4 cup heatproof glass measuring cup. Add the bourbon and peppermint extract and stir to incorporate.

5. Place 6 flameproof 7-ounce custard cups or ramekins into the water in the baking pan. Pour an equal amount of the custard into the cups. Bake for about 1 hour, or until just set. (Rotate the baking pan 180 degrees halfway through the baking time.) The top of the custards should still slightly shake; the custard will completely set when chilled.

6. Remove the custard cups from the baking pan, and place them on a wire rack until cool, about 30 minutes. Cover each custard cup with plastic wrap and refrigerate for 3 to 4 hours before serving.

continued

7. To serve, preheat the broiler. Remove the chilled custards from the refrigerator; remove and discard the plastic wrap. Place the custard cups on a baking sheet and evenly sprinkle the top of each custard with 1 teaspoon sugar. Position the baking sheet on the center rack under the broiler and broil until the sugar is caramelized to a dark amber. Refrigerate the custards for a few minutes to firm the caramelized sugar before serving. Garnish each with a mint sprig, if desired.

THE CHEF'S TOUCH

Steeping the vanilla bean in the cream imbues the custard with a wonderful flavor and aroma. If you don't have a bean, substitute 2 teaspoons pure vanilla extract for acceptable results, adding it with the bourbon and peppermint extract.

The baked custard component of the crème brûlée will keep in the refrigerator for 2 to 3 days, making it a great dessert for a dinner party. Caramelize the sugar tops just a few minutes before serving.

At the Trellis we use a propane torch to caramelize the sugar. If that sounds like fun, you can get your torch at the hardware store (and you'll find you have more control over the results of the caramelized sugar).

If you choose to use heatproof glass cups, as we did for the photograph, it is imperative to use a propane torch rather than caramelizing under the broiler.

Overindulgence is not in my vocabulary. But if the size of the portion seems too decadent you can use 4-ounce custard cups and increase the number of servings (you should get nine). Baking time will be 50 minutes rather than 1 hour.

caramel chocolate chip cake

SERVES 10 TO 12

The kid in a lot of us will love this cake. With the same synergy as Santa and reindeer, chocolate and caramel deliver a treasure trove of joyful flavor and texture. Add Caramel Chocolate Chip Cake for everyone on your list (and check it twice so you don't disappoint).

CARAMEL CHOCOLATE CHIP CAKE

8 ounces (2 sticks) unsalted butter, cut into 1-tablespoon pieces, plus 1 tablespoon, melted

1¾ cups all-purpose flour

½ teaspoon baking powder

⅛ teaspoon salt

2 cups tightly packed dark brown sugar

4 large eggs

½ cup buttermilk

1 teaspoon pure vanilla extract

1½ cups Nestlé Milk Chocolate & Caramel Swirled® Morsels, or the same amount semisweet chocolate chips

DARK CHOCOLATE GANACHE AND GARNISH

14 ounces semisweet baking chocolate, coarsely chopped

4 ounces unsweetened baking chocolate, coarsely chopped

2⅓ cups heavy cream

1 tablespoon plus 1½ teaspoons granulated sugar

½ cup Nestlé Milk Chocolate & Caramel Swirled Morsels or semisweet chocolate chips

MAKE THE CARAMEL CHOCOLATE CHIP CAKE:

1. Preheat the oven to 350°F. Lightly coat three 9 × 1½-inch round cake pans with the melted 1 tablespoon butter. Line the bottom of the pans with parchment or wax paper.

2. In a sifter, combine the flour, baking powder, and salt. Sift onto a large piece of parchment or wax paper.

3. Place the brown sugar and 8 ounces butter in the bowl of a stand electric mixer fitted with a paddle. Mix on the lowest speed for 1 minute, then beat on medium for 2 minutes. Stop and scrape down the sides of the bowl and paddle. Beat on medium-high for 2 minutes, until very soft. Scrape down again. Add the eggs one at a time, beating on medium for 30 seconds after each addition; scrape down again once all the eggs have been incorporated. Beat on medium for 30 seconds more. Turn the mixer on low and gradually add the dry ingredients; mix about 15 seconds until incorporated. Scrape down again.

4. Add the buttermilk and vanilla and mix on the lowest speed to combine, then add the milk chocolate–caramel morsels and mix until incorporated, about 10 seconds. Remove the bowl from the mixer, and use a rubber spatula to finish mixing the ingredients until thoroughly combined. Immediately divide the batter among the prepared pans, spreading it evenly with the rubber spatula. Bake on the top and center racks of the oven until a toothpick inserted in the center of each layer comes out clean, about 24 minutes. (Switch the pans between top and center and rotate each 180 degrees halfway through the baking time.) Remove the cake layers from the oven and cool in the pans for 10 minutes at room temperature.

continued

5. Cover 3 cake circles with parchment or wax paper. Use a paring knife to cut between the cake and the inside edge of the pan and invert the cake layers onto the cake circles. Carefully peel the paper away from the bottom of each layer. Refrigerate the cake layers uncovered.

MAKE THE DARK CHOCOLATE GANACHE AND ASSEMBLE THE CAKE:

6. Place the chopped chocolates in a large heatproof bowl. Bring the cream and granulated sugar to a boil in a small saucepan over medium-high heat, stirring to dissolve the sugar. Pour the cream over the chocolate and stir with a whisk until smooth.

7. Measure out 2¼ cups of the ganache and spread evenly on a baking sheet with sides with a rubber spatula. Refrigerate the baking sheet for 15 to 20 minutes until the ganache is slightly firm. Keep the remaining ¾ cups of ganache at room temperature.

8. Remove the cake layers and the ganache from the refrigerator. Use an icing spatula to spread ¾ cup of the chilled ganache evenly and smoothly over the top and sides of one of the layers. Place the second layer (baked top down) on the ganache and gently press it into place. Use an icing spatula to spread ¾ cup of the chilled ganache evenly and smoothly over the top and sides of the second layer. Place the third layer (also baked top down) on the second layer, and gently press it into place.

9. Use an icing spatula to spread the remaining chilled ganache evenly and smoothly over the top and sides of the third layer. Refrigerate the cake for 15 minutes.

10. Remove the cake from the refrigerator and pour the reserved room-temperature ganache over the top of the cake; use an icing spatula to spread the ganache smoothly and evenly over the top and sides of the cake. Sprinkle the milk chocolate–caramel morsels evenly over the top of the cake. Refrigerate the cake for 2 hours before serving.

11. To serve, heat the blade of a serrated knife under hot running water and wipe dry before cutting each slice. Keep the slices at room temperature for 15 to 20 minutes before serving.

THE CHEF'S TOUCH

The choice between milk chocolate–caramel morsels and regular semisweet chocolate chips depends on the age of your cake eaters: Younger kids may prefer the sweeter milk chocolate–caramel morsels; the intense chocolate flavor of regular semisweet chocolate chips would no doubt appeal to a more mature palate. Either way, the dynamic caramel flavor derived from the brown sugar will satisfy anyone's caramel cravings.

After assembly, you may keep the Caramel Chocolate Chip Cake in the refrigerator for 2 to 3 days. To prevent the cake from absorbing refrigerator odors, store it in a tightly sealed plastic container.

chocolate cherry cheesecake

SERVES 10 TO 12

For many adults, the maraschino cherry comes to the party merely as a garnish in a cocktail. If this is your case, then prepare yourself for maraschino madness. The flavor and color achieved by using the much-maligned maraschino would not happen with fresh cherries. Besides, if you're baking this for the Christmas holiday, fresh cherries would be difficult to locate. So here's wishing you a cherry Christmas and don't be a snob, enjoy!

SWEET AND SOUR SUGAR CHERRY FLAVORED COOKIE CRUST

¼ cup all-purpose flour

Sweet and Sour Sugar Cookies (cherry-flavored option; see Santa's Workshop, page 169), unbaked

1 tablespoon unsalted butter, melted

CHERRY CHEESECAKE FILLING

Three 8-ounce packages cream cheese, softened

1 cup granulated sugar

6 large eggs

1 cup maraschino cherries, coarsely chopped

2 tablespoons maraschino cherry juice

CHOCOLATE GANACHE AND GARNISH

12 ounces semisweet baking chocolate, coarsely chopped

4 ounces unsweetened baking chocolate, coarsely chopped

2 cups heavy cream

2 tablespoons granulated sugar

10 to 12 whole maraschino cherries with stems, patted dry

MAKE THE SWEET AND SOUR SUGAR CHERRY FLAVORED COOKIE CRUST:

1. Preheat the oven to 325°F.

2. Lightly flour a clean, dry work surface with some of the flour. Weigh out and transfer 6 ounces of the dough to the work surface and knead gently to form a smooth ball. (The remaining dough can be frozen or baked into cookies.) Wrap the dough in plastic wrap and refrigerate for 20 minutes.

3. While the dough is chilling, coat a 9 × 3–inch springform pan with the melted butter. Remove the dough from the refrigerator, and remove and discard the plastic wrap. Sprinkle more flour on the work surface as necessary. Place the dough on the work surface. Dust a rolling pin with some of the flour and roll the dough into a circle 9 inches in diameter and ⅛ inch thick. Line the bottom of the springform pan with the dough, gently pressing the dough into the bottom. Bake on the center rack of the oven for 20 minutes. Remove from the oven and set aside at room temperature.

continued

MAKE THE CHERRY CHEESECAKE FILLING:

4. Lower the oven temperature to 300°F.

5. Place the cream cheese and sugar in the bowl of a stand electric mixer fitted with a paddle. Beat on low for 1 minute, on medium for 1 minute, and on high for 1 minute. Stop and scrape down the sides of the bowl. Mix again on high for 30 seconds (the batter should be very soft). Scrape down again. Add the eggs two at a time, beating on medium for 15 seconds after each addition, and scrape down again once all of the eggs have been incorporated. Add the chopped cherries and cherry juice, then beat on medium for 15 seconds. Remove the bowl from the mixer, and use a rubber spatula to finish mixing the batter until it is thoroughly combined.

6. Pour the filling over the crust in the springform pan.

7. Cover the top of the pan with aluminum foil and bake on the center rack of the oven. Remove the foil after 1 hour, and bake until the filling reaches 170°F, about 1 hour more. Use a digital thermometer (see Equipment, page 186) for an accurate reading. Remove the cheesecake from the oven and cool at room temperature for 1 hour. Refrigerate the cheesecake for at least 12 hours before making the ganache (do not remove the cake from the pan).

MAKE THE CHOCOLATE GANACHE AND DECORATE:

8. Place the chocolates in a large heatproof bowl. Bring the cream and sugar to a boil in a medium saucepan over medium heat, stirring to dissolve the sugar. Pour the cream over the chocolates; stir with a whisk until smooth. Set aside.

9. To release the cheesecake from the springform pan, wrap a damp, hot towel around the sides of the pan. Make sure the towel covers the sides completely. Hold the towel around the pan for about 1 minute, then carefully release and remove the springform sides. If the top surface edges of the cheesecake is not level, trim it with a serrated knife. Line a baking sheet with parchment or wax paper. Use a wide utility turner to remove the cheesecake from the pan and place it onto the baking sheet with sides. Ladle 1¾ cups of the ganache over the top of the cheesecake. Use an icing spatula to spread a smooth coating of ganache over the top and sides of the cheesecake. Refrigerate the cheesecake for 15 to 20 minutes until the ganache is firm.

10. Remove the cheesecake from the refrigerator and pour the remaining ganache over the top, and use an icing spatula to spread the second coat of ganache over the top and sides. Decorate the top of the cheesecake with the maraschino cherries. Refrigerate the cheesecake for at least 2 hours before serving.

11. To serve, heat the blade of a serrated knife under hot running water and wipe dry before cutting each slice.

THE CHEF'S TOUCH

If you have been standoffish about eating maraschino cherries because of the red dye that gives them the intense color, put your fears to rest. Today's maraschinos use the same harmless dye used safely in chewing gum and other foods—not the carcinogenic red dye #3 of days gone by.

Ever wonder what gives the red maraschino cherry its unique taste? Wonder no more—it is almond extract!

If you have forgotten to soften the cream cheese to room temperature, unwrap it and pop it in the microwave for about 30 seconds.

After assembly, you may keep the cheesecake in the refrigerator for 2 to 3 days before serving. To prevent the cheesecake from absorbing refrigerator odors, store it in a tightly sealed plastic container.

chocolate mandarin truffle cake

SERVES 8 TO 10

So sensuous is this confection that an apt description may not be appropriate for a cookbook. Without a speck of flour to weigh the cake down, orange and chocolate rendezvous and produce a chocolate velvet nirvana that feels as good in your mouth as it tastes.

TRUFFLE CAKE

12 ounces (3 sticks) unsalted butter, cut into 1-tablespoon pieces, plus 1 tablespoon, melted

1½ pounds semisweet baking chocolate, coarsely chopped

9 large eggs

2 tablespoons thin julienne orange zest (see The Chef's Touch, page 144)

1 tablespoon pure orange extract

CITRUS ICING

1 pound (4 sticks) unsalted butter cut into 1-tablespoon pieces

1 tablespoon finely minced orange zest

1 pound confectioners' sugar, sifted

2 tablespoons heavy cream

2 tablespoons fresh orange juice

1 teaspoon orange extract

GARNISH (OPTIONAL)

Peeled, seeded fresh tangerine sections or julienne candied orange peel

MAKE THE TRUFFLE CAKE:

1. Preheat the oven to 325°F. Lightly coat two 9 × 1½-inch round cake pans with some of the melted 1 tablespoon butter. Line the bottom of the pans with parchment or wax paper, then lightly coat the paper with more melted butter.

2. Melt the chocolate and 12 ounces butter in the top of a double boiler or in a large glass bowl in a microwave oven (see Techniques, page 191), and stir until smooth.

3. Place the eggs, julienne orange zest, and orange extract in the bowl of a stand electric mixer fitted with a paddle. Mix on medium-high for 3 minutes until slightly thickened and pale in color. Add the melted chocolate and mix on medium for 2 minutes until thoroughly incorporated. Remove the bowl from the mixer, and use a rubber spatula to finish mixing the batter until completely smooth and incorporated. Immediately divide the cake batter between the prepared cake pans, spreading it evenly with a rubber spatula.

4. Bake on the center rack of the oven until a toothpick inserted in the center of each layer comes out clean, about 25 minutes. Remove the cake layers from the oven and cool in the pans for 2 to 3 minutes, until the pans can be handled with bare hands. Invert the cake layers onto cake circles or cake plates. Carefully peel the paper away

continued

from the cake layers. Refrigerate the cake layers, uncovered, while making the Citrus Icing.

MAKE THE CITRUS ICING:

5. Place the butter and minced orange zest in the bowl of a stand electric mixer fitted with a paddle. Mix on low for 1 minute, then increase the speed to medium-high and beat for 2 minutes until soft. Stop and scrape down the sides of the bowl and the paddle. Beat on medium for 2 minutes more until very soft. Add the confectioners' sugar and mix on the lowest speed to combine, about 1 minute. Scrape down again. Add the cream, orange juice, and orange extract, mix on low for 10 seconds, then beat on medium-high for 1 minute. Remove the bowl from the mixer, and use a rubber spatula to finish mixing the icing until thoroughly incorporated.

ASSEMBLE THE CAKE AND SERVE:

6. Remove the cakes from the refrigerator. Turn one of the cakes baked top up. Use an icing spatula to evenly and smoothly spread 2 cups of the icing over the top, to the edge. Place the second inverted layer (baked top down) on the icing and gently press it into place. Use a small serrated knife to trim away any rough edges around the cake. Spread the remaining icing on the top and sides of the cake. Refrigerate the cake for 1 hour before serving.

7. Heat the blade of a serrated knife under hot running water and wipe dry before cutting each slice. Keep the slices at room temperature for 15 to 20 minutes before serving. Garnish with tangerine sections or julienne candied orange peel, if desired, for a festive touch.

THE CHEF'S TOUCH

For the julienne orange zest, use a sharp vegetable peeler to remove the colored part of the skin, not the bitter white pith underneath. Once you have removed the colored skin, use a very sharp cook's knife to cut the skin into as thin slivers as possible.

Do not leave the cake layers in the pans for more than the short time it takes for the pans to be cool enough to handle; otherwise, they will be difficult to extract.

Handle the baked cake layers with care. Due to the absence of flour, the cakes are very dense and not flexible.

The assembled cake may be kept in the refrigerator for up to 3 days before serving. To prevent the cake from absorbing refrigerator odors, store it in a tightly sealed plastic container. This container is also great for transporting the cake to a Christmas celebration at someone else's home. Then again, you may want to reserve something this decadent for the privacy of your own home.

white chocolate cranberry cake

SERVES 8 TO 10

Mention Christmas colors and most people think red and green. Thanks to snowy holidays in New England where I grew up, I always envision white on that palette. Now I'm a Virginian; I envision white chocolate on the palate! White chocolate mousse cake, like a blissfully moist snowfall, greets the season with a cheerfully adorned cranberry icing. May all your Christmases be white (chocolate).

WHITE CHOCOLATE MOUSSE CAKE

4 tablespoons (½ stick) unsalted butter, cut into 1-tablespoon pieces, plus 1 tablespoon, melted

12 ounces white chocolate, coarsely chopped

10 large egg yolks

¾ cup granulated sugar

1 teaspoon pure vanilla extract

½ cup all-purpose flour

6 large egg whites

CRANBERRY ICING

1½ cups fresh or thawed frozen whole cranberries

1½ pounds (6 sticks) unsalted butter, cut into 1-tablespoon pieces, softened

3 tablespoons Black Duck Premium Cranberry Liqueur

2½ cups confectioners' sugar, sifted

MAKE THE WHITE CHOCOLATE MOUSSE CAKE:

1. Preheat the oven to 325°F. Lightly coat three 9 × 1½–inch round cake pans with some of the melted 1 tablespoon butter. Line the bottoms of the pans with parchment or wax paper, then lightly coat the paper with more melted butter.

2. Melt the chocolate and 4 tablespoons butter in the top of a double boiler or in a medium glass bowl in a microwave oven (see Techniques, page 191), and stir until smooth.

3. Place the egg yolks, ½ cup of the granulated sugar, and the vanilla in the bowl of a stand electric mixer fitted with a paddle. Beat on high until lemon-colored and slightly thickened, about 4 minutes. Add the melted white chocolate and beat on medium-high until thoroughly combined, about 30 seconds. Remove the bowl from the mixer. Use a rubber spatula to fold in the flour. Transfer the mixture to a large bowl and set aside.

4. Place the egg whites in the clean bowl of a stand electric mixer fitted with a balloon whip (the bowl and the whip need to be meticulously clean and dry; otherwise, the egg whites will not whisk properly). Whisk on high for 45 seconds until soft peaks form, then gradually add the remaining ¼ cup granulated sugar and continue to whisk on high until stiff peaks form, about 45 seconds. Remove the bowl from the mixer. Add about a third of the egg whites to the egg yolk mixture and fold to incorporate, using a rubber spatula. Add the remaining egg whites and fold until the mixture is uniform in color. Immediately divide the batter into the prepared pans, spreading it evenly with a rubber spatula.

continued

5. Bake on the top and center racks of the oven until a toothpick inserted in the center of each layer comes out clean, 21 to 22 minutes. (Switch the pans between top and center and rotate each pan 180 degrees halfway through the baking time.) Remove the cake layers from the oven, and cool in the pans at room temperature for 30 minutes. Invert the cake layers onto cake circles or cake plates. Carefully peel the paper away from the bottom of each layer, then turn the layers baked top up. Refrigerate the cake layers uncovered.

MAKE THE CRANBERRY ICING:

6. If using fresh cranberries, place them on a baking sheet with sides and into a 325°F oven for about 8 minutes, until the cranberries burst, then refrigerate the cranberries. This step is not necessary if using thawed frozen cranberries.

7. Place the butter in the bowl of a stand electric mixer fitted with a paddle. Mix on low for 1 minute; increase the speed to medium and beat for 1 minute. Use a rubber spatula to scrape down the sides of the bowl and the paddle. Add the cranberries and mix on the lowest speed for 15 seconds; increase the speed to medium and beat for 1 minute. Stop and scrape down the sides of the bowl and the paddle. Beat on medium-high for 1 more minute until very soft. Scrape down again. Add the cranberry liqueur, then gradually add the confectioners' sugar while mixing on the lowest speed until combined, about 1½ minutes. Scrape down again. Beat on medium-high for 1 minute more until very soft and fluffy. Remove the bowl from the mixer, and use a rubber spatula to finish mixing the icing until thoroughly combined.

ASSEMBLE THE CAKE AND SERVE:

8. Remove the cake layers from the refrigerator. Fit a pastry bag with a large star tip. Transfer 1 cup of the icing to the pastry bag and set aside at room temperature. Use an icing spatula to evenly spread 1 cup of the remaining icing over the top of one of the cake layers, to the edge. Use a wide utility turner to remove the second layer from its cake circle and place it on the icing. Spread another cup of icing over the top of the second layer, to the edge. Top with the last cake layer. Gently press the layers into place. Use a sharp serrated knife to trim any rough edges around the cake. Spread the remaining icing evenly over the top and sides of the cake.

9. Use the pastry bag to pipe a ring of 8 to 10 evenly spaced cranberry icing stars (about ¾ inch high and 1½ inches wide) along the outside edge of the top of the cake. Refrigerate the cake for at least 1 hour before cutting and serving.

10. Heat the blade of a serrated knife under hot water and wipe dry before cutting each slice. Slice the cake while still cold, then keep the slices at room temperature for 30 minutes before serving (this will greatly enhance the flavor).

THE CHEF'S TOUCH

With only a scant half cup of flour, this exquisitely light cake delivers sweet indulgence, perfectly balanced by a vibrantly tart cranberry icing, which makes it the perfect choice for your holiday table.

As an additional adornment, garnish the top of the icing stars with whole thawed frozen cranberries that have been rolled in granulated sugar.

After assembly, you may keep the White Chocolate Cranberry Cake in the refrigerator for 2 days. To prevent the cake from absorbing refrigerator odors, store it in a tightly sealed plastic container.

This cake may be prepared over 2 days:

day 1: Bake the White Chocolate Mousse Cake layers; once cooled, cover with plastic wrap and refrigerate overnight.

day 2: Make the Cranberry Icing, assemble the cake as directed, and refrigerate for 1 hour before serving.

chocolate buttons up buttershots bundt cake

SERVES 12

"Buttons up" to a confection that is easily prepared yet delivers incomparable flavor. The surprisingly harmonious partnership of chocolate and butterscotch elicits the "WOW!" that will make this Bundt cake a new holiday classic.

8 ounces (2 sticks) unsalted butter, cut into 1-tablespoon pieces and softened, plus 1 tablespoon, melted

1¾ cups all-purpose flour

¾ teaspoon baking powder

¼ teaspoon salt

1 cup granulated sugar

2 large eggs

6 ounces semisweet baking chocolate, melted (see Techniques, page 191)

½ cup buttermilk

½ cup DeKuyper® Buttershots® Schnapps or butterscotch-flavored liqueur

1 cup butterscotch morsels

GARNISH

Butterscotch Sauce (see Santa's Workshop, page 175)

Unsweetened whipped cream, optional

1. Preheat the oven to 350°F. Liberally coat a 12-cup nonstick Bundt pan with the melted 1 tablespoon butter, making sure that all of the indentations in the pan are completely coated. Place the pan in the freezer until needed. (The Bundt pan needs to be very cold to allow the butter to adhere to the nonstick surface; this will facilitate removal of the baked cake.)

2. In a sifter, combine the flour, baking powder, and salt. Sift onto a large piece of parchment or wax paper.

3. Place the sugar and the remaining butter in the bowl of a stand electric mixer fitted with a paddle. Mix on the lowest speed for 1 minute, then beat on medium for 1 minute. Stop and scrape down the sides of the bowl. Beat on medium-high for 1 minute, until very soft. Scrape down again. Add the eggs one at a time, beating on medium for 30 seconds after each addition and scraping down once all the eggs have been incorporated.

4. Beat on medium for 30 seconds more. Add the chocolate and beat on medium for 15 to 20 seconds until incorporated. Scrape down again. Turn the mixer on to low and gradually add the dry ingredients; mix until incorporated, about 30 seconds. Scrape down again. Very gradually add the buttermilk, followed by the schnapps, and mix on low to incorporate, about 30 seconds. Remove the bowl from the mixer, and use a rubber spatula to fold the butterscotch morsels into the batter until thoroughly combined.

continued

5. Remove the Bundt pan from the freezer. Use a rubber spatula to transfer the batter into the pan, spreading evenly. Bake on the center rack of the oven until a toothpick inserted in the center of the cake comes out clean, about 55 minutes. Remove from the oven, and cool in the pan at room temperature for 5 minutes. Invert the cake onto a cooling rack (the longer the cake stays in the pan, the more difficult it will be to release it from the pan). Cool the cake at room temperature for 25 to 30 minutes, then place it in a tightly sealed plastic container and refrigerate for 1 hour before slicing and serving.

6. Heat the blade of a serrated knife under hot running water and wipe dry before cutting each slice. Serve accompanied by the Butterscotch Sauce and a cloud or two of unsweetened whipped cream if desired.

THE CHEF'S TOUCH

This Chocolate Buttons Up Buttershots Bundt Cake may be unadorned, but the flavor is fanciful. Originally I was tempted to bathe the whole cake in ganache. But my first bite—which was interrupted by "WOW!"—dissuaded me from any further embellishment.

Talking about flavor, we have also made this cake using semisweet chocolate morsels rather than the butterscotch. Inconceivably delicious!

This cake may be kept in a tightly sealed plastic container in the refrigerator for several days. I prefer to eat this particular cake directly from the refrigerator, rather than at room temperature. The cake may also be frozen for several weeks. To prevent the cake from absorbing freezer odors, store it in a tightly sealed plastic container. Thaw the cake in the refrigerator before serving.

chocolate gingerbread cake

SERVES 8 TO 10

Every bite of this agreeable cake sings like a Christmas carol. The flavor of gingerbread, although not exclusive to Christmas, is certainly synonymous with that merry time of the year. Can't you just hear "All I want for Christmas is Chocolate Gingerbread Cake" as the chocolate and ginger aromas waft through your kitchen?

CHOCOLATE GINGERBREAD CAKE

6 tablespoons (¾ stick) unsalted butter, cut into 1-tablespoon pieces and softened, plus 2 tablespoons, melted

1¾ cups all-purpose flour

1 teaspoon baking soda

⅛ teaspoon salt

¼ teaspoon ground ginger

⅛ teaspoon ground cinnamon

Pinch of ground cloves

¾ cup warm water (100° to 110°F)

1½ cups tightly packed light brown sugar

2 large eggs

1 large egg yolk

2 ounces unsweetened baking chocolate, melted (see Techniques, page 191)

¾ cup sour cream

CHOCOLATE GINGER BUTTERCREAM

6 ounces semisweet baking chocolate, coarsely chopped

2 ounces unsweetened baking chocolate, coarsely chopped

1 cup heavy cream

¼ cup granulated sugar

½ teaspoon ground ginger

¼ teaspoon ground cinnamon

8 ounces (2 sticks) unsalted butter, cut into 1-tablespoon pieces and softened

GARNISH (OPTIONAL)

8 to 10 pieces crystallized ginger

MAKE THE CHOCOLATE GINGERBREAD CAKE:

1. Preheat the oven to 325°F. Liberally coat two 9 × 1½–inch round cake pans with some of the melted
2 tablespoons butter. Line the bottom of the pans with parchment or wax paper, then coat the paper with more melted butter.

2. In a sifter, combine the flour, baking soda, and salt. Sift onto a large piece of parchment or wax paper.

3. Place the ginger, cinnamon, and cloves in a small bowl. Pour the warm water over the spices and whisk to incorporate.

4. Place the remaining butter and the brown sugar in the bowl of a stand electric mixer fitted with a paddle. Mix on low for 1 minute, then on medium for 1 minute more. Stop and scrape down the sides of the bowl and the paddle. Beat on medium-high

continued

for 1 minute, then scrape down again. Add the eggs and egg yolk, one at a time, beating on medium for 30 seconds after each addition and scraping down once all the eggs have been incorporated. Add the melted chocolate, and beat on medium for 15 seconds until thoroughly incorporated. Turn the mixer on to low and gradually add the dry ingredients; mix until incorporated, about 30 seconds. Scrape down again. Add the sour cream and mix on low for 15 seconds. Gradually add the spiced water and mix on low for 15 seconds, then beat on medium for 15 seconds until thoroughly incorporated. Remove the bowl from the mixer, and use a rubber spatula to finish mixing the batter until thoroughly combined.

5. Immediately divide the batter into the prepared pans, spreading evenly with a rubber spatula. Bake on the center rack of the oven until a toothpick inserted into the center of each layer comes out clean, about 30 minutes. Remove from the oven, and cool in the pans at room temperature for 10 minutes. Cover 2 cake circles with plastic wrap and invert the cake layers onto the circles (the plastic wrap prevents the somewhat sticky cake layers from adhering to the circles). Carefully peel the paper away from the bottom of each layer. Refrigerate the cake layers, uncovered, for at least 1 hour before assembling.

MAKE THE CHOCOLATE GINGER BUTTERCREAM:

6. Place the chocolates in a medium heatproof bowl. Bring the heavy cream, granulated sugar, ginger, and cinnamon to a boil in a medium saucepan over medium-high heat, stirring to dissolve the sugar. Pour the mixture over the chocolate and stir with a whisk until smooth (voilà—this is ganache). Pour the ganache onto a baking sheet with sides, and refrigerate until slightly chilled but not firm, about 20 minutes.

7. Place the butter in the bowl of a stand electric mixer fitted with a paddle. Mix on low for 1 minute, then beat on medium for 2 minutes. Stop and scrape down the sides of the bowl and the paddle. Beat on medium-high for 1 minute, until very soft. Scrape down again. Add the chilled ganache, and beat on medium for 30 seconds. Scrape down again, then beat on medium for 30 seconds more until thoroughly combined. Transfer ½ cup of the buttercream to a pastry bag fitted with a large star tip.

ASSEMBLE THE CAKE AND SERVE:

8. Remove the cake layers from the refrigerator. Use an icing spatula to evenly spread 1 cup of buttercream over the top and to the edges of one of the inverted cake layers. Place the second layer, baked top up, on the icing and gently press into place. Spread the remaining buttercream smoothly onto the top and sides of the cake. Pipe an evenly spaced ring of 8 to 10 buttercream stars (about ¾ inch high and 1½ inches wide) along the outside edge of the top of the cake. If desired, place a piece of crystallized ginger on each star. Refrigerate the cake for 2 hours before slicing and serving.

9. Heat the blade of a serrated knife under hot running water and wipe dry before cutting each slice. Keep the slices at room temperature for 15 to 20 minutes before serving.

THE CHEF'S TOUCH

The Chocolate Gingerbread Cake needs no further adornment, but in the holiday spirit you could place miniature gingerbread cookies (see the recipe for Chocolate Gingerbread Snowflakes, page 118) adjacent to each buttercream star.

After assembly, you may keep the Chocolate Gingerbread Cake in the refrigerator for 3 to 4 days. To prevent the cake from absorbing refrigerator odors, store it in a tightly sealed plastic container.

chocolate hazelnut elagantes

MAKES 6 ELAGANTES

Elagantes are so swellagante! So beautiful to the eyes, and even more astonishing with every bite, this multilayered confection delivers a suave blend of textures and flavors. Chocolate and hazelnuts, the dominant theme, make a match certain to impress at your next intimate holiday dinner party.

HAZELNUT MERINGUES

2 large egg whites

Pinch of cream of tartar

½ cup granulated sugar

¼ cup hazelnuts, skinned, toasted (see Techniques, page 192), and coarsely chopped

HAZELNUT BARK

10 ounces semisweet baking chocolate

½ cup hazelnuts, skinned, toasted, and coarsely chopped

DARK CHOCOLATE MOUSSE

2 ounces semisweet baking chocolate, coarsely chopped

2 ounces unsweetened baking chocolate, coarsely chopped

1½ cups heavy cream

2 tablespoons granulated sugar

1 tablespoon Frangelico

DARK CHOCOLATE GANACHE AND GARNISH

1½ pounds semisweet baking chocolate, coarsely chopped

3 cups heavy cream

¼ cup Frangelico

¾ cup hazelnuts, skinned, toasted (see Techniques, page 192), and coarsely chopped

2 ounces white chocolate, melted (see Techniques, page 191)

Frangelico Cream Sauce (see Santa's Workshop, page 174), for serving

MAKE THE HAZELNUT MERINGUES:

1. Preheat the oven to 225°F.

2. Using a 3½-inch round cookie cutter as a guide, use a pencil to trace 6 evenly spaced circles on a piece of parchment paper cut to fit a baking sheet. Place the sheet of parchment paper on the baking sheet, trace marks face down.

3. Place the egg whites and cream of tartar in the bowl of a stand electric mixer fitted with a balloon whip. Whisk on high until stiff peaks form, about 1 minute and 30 seconds. Gradually pour in the sugar in a slow, steady stream while whisking on high for about 15 seconds until the sugar is absorbed and the egg whites have formed soft peaks. Remove the bowl from the mixer, and use a rubber spatula to fold in the hazelnuts until combined.

4. Fill a pastry bag (with no tip) with the meringue batter. Anchor the parchment onto the baking sheets with a tiny dab of meringue under each

continued

corner (this will keep the parchment from fluttering up during baking). Fill each traced circle with the meringue: start in the center and pipe a ½-inch-wide spiral toward the outside of the circle. Place the baking sheet on the center rack of the oven and bake for 1 hour, until dry. Remove from the oven and allow to cool on the baking sheet for 30 minutes before handling.

MAKE THE HAZELNUT BARK:

5. Line a baking sheet with sides with parchment or wax paper.

6. Melt the semisweet chocolate in the top of a double boiler or in a medium glass bowl in a microwave oven (see Techniques, page 191) and stir until smooth. Use a rubber spatula to fold in the hazelnuts. Transfer the mixture to the baking sheet, and use the spatula to spread it as evenly as possible toward the edge. Refrigerate for 10 minutes, until slightly firm.

7. Remove the bark from the refrigerator. Use a 3½-inch round cookie cutter to cut 6 circles from the bark. Do not remove the circles yet, but refrigerate on the pan until needed.

MAKE THE DARK CHOCOLATE MOUSSE:

8. Place the chocolates in a medium heatproof bowl. Bring ½ cup of the cream and the sugar to a boil in a small saucepan over medium heat, stirring to dissolve the sugar. Remove from the heat, add the Frangelico, and immediately pour the cream over the chocolate. Whisk vigorously until smooth. Set aside at room temperature.

9. Place the remaining 1 cup cream in the bowl of a stand electric mixer fitted with a balloon whip. Whisk on high until stiff peaks form, about 1 minute and 15 seconds. Remove the bowl from the mixer, and use a rubber spatula to fold in the chocolate mixture until thoroughly incorporated and smooth. (Don't be concerned that at this point the mousse resembles cake batter; it will set firm with refrigeration.) Cover the bowl with plastic wrap, and refrigerate for at least 30 minutes.

MAKE THE DARK CHOCOLATE GANACHE:

10. Place the semisweet chocolate in a large heatproof bowl. Bring the cream to a boil in a medium saucepan over medium heat. Remove from the heat and add the Frangelico, then pour the cream over the chocolate and stir with a whisk until smooth.

ASSEMBLE AND DECORATE THE ELAGANTES:

11. Wrap the bottom inserts of six 6 × 1½–inch nonstick springform pans with plastic wrap (the plastic wrap will allow easy removal of the assembled Elagantes), then assemble the pans with the bottom inserts turned over (the lip of the inserts facing down).

12. Line the inside of each pan with a 13 × 3½–inch strip of parchment or wax paper.

13. Remove the hazelnut bark from the refrigerator, and separate the circles from the chocolate "scraps" (the "scraps" make for fine munching). Place a bark circle in the bottom of each pan.

14. Remove the Dark Chocolate Mousse from the refrigerator. Portion 5 tablespoons or 1 slightly heaping #12 ice-cream scoop of the mousse on top of each piece of bark, spreading evenly with the back of a dessert spoon. Place a meringue on top of the chocolate mousse in each pan and gently press down. Portion a level #12 ice-cream scoop of the Dark Chocolate Ganache over the meringues in each pan. Place the Elagantes in the freezer for 1 hour.

15. Remove the Elagantes from the freezer. Release the springform pan sides. Transfer the Elagantes to a cooling rack set on a baking sheet with sides. Remove the paper sleeves. Ladle an equal amount (¾ cup) of Dark Chocolate Ganache over each Elagante, allowing the ganache to flow over the top and sides, then refrigerate for at least 30 minutes before decorating.

16. Press the coarsely chopped hazelnuts into the sides of each Elagante, coating the sides evenly.

17. Transfer the melted white chocolate to a small resealable plastic bag. Snip about ⅛ inch from one bottom corner of the bag. Pipe zigzag lines of white chocolate over the top of each Elagante. Refrigerate for 30 minutes before serving. Serve the Elagantes cold, accompanied by the Frangelico Cream Sauce.

THE CHEF'S TOUCH

The culinary word for the classic combination of chocolate and hazelnuts is *gianduja* (zhahn-doo-yah), an utterly unutterable name for an unbelievably, unimaginably delicious marriage.

Handle the baked meringues with care to avoid breakage. If the meringue breaks, you can still use it (it will not be noticed in the assembled dessert unless it is smashed into bits).

Turning over the bottom insert of the springform pan (the lip of the bottom insert facing down) before assembling the pan makes it easier to remove the insert from the assembled Elagante.

Once the Elagantes have been assembled and decorated, they should be served within 24 hours; otherwise the baked meringue will lose its crispness. If you plan to keep the assembled Elagantes in the refrigerator beyond 30 minutes, place them in a tightly sealed plastic container so that they do not absorb refrigerator odors.

refuge of chocolate pistachio mousse

MAKES 6 SERVINGS

Chocolate Pistachio Mousse, although prosaic in its preparation, has found a fetching repository in the accompanying chocolate "refuge." The scintillating cylinder of dark chocolate is indeed exquisite, making this the perfect fashionable holiday dessert.

CHOCOLATE REFUGE

12 ounces high-quality semisweet chocolate (preferably with a high percentage of cocoa solids), coarsely chopped

CHOCOLATE PISTACHIO MOUSSE

10 ounces semisweet baking chocolate, coarsely chopped

2 ounces unsweetened baking chocolate, coarsely chopped

2 ¼ cups heavy cream

5 large egg whites

1 cup shelled pistachios, skinned, toasted (see The Chef's Touch, page 160, and Techniques, page 192), and each cut in half

GARNISH

White Chocolate Spiced Rum Sauce (see Santa's Workshop, page 182)

MAKE THE CHOCOLATE REFUGES:

1. Cover a clean, dry, flat work surface with a large piece of parchment paper; line a baking sheet with parchment. Place six 12 × 3–inch strips of parchment paper on the work surface (the parchment sheet covering comes in handy for clean-up, as you will see).

2. Melt the semisweet chocolate in the top of a double boiler or in a medium glass bowl in a microwave oven (see Techniques, page 191), and stir until smooth.

3. Transfer half of the melted chocolate into a small resealable plastic bag. Snip about ⅛ inch from the bottom corner of the bag. Pipe zigzag lines of chocolate onto about ¾ of the length of each individual strip of parchment paper until you have created a lattice-like appearance.

4. Lay out six 3-inch diameter (inside), 2½-inch-long PVC pipes. Picking up the paper strips by the end of the paper without chocolate, one at a time carefully line the inside of each pipe with the chocolate-latticed parchment (the plain side of the paper should be in contact with the pipe, not the chocolate side). Be careful that the paper does not flop inward.

5. Refrigerate the pipes on the baking sheet until the chocolate has hardened, about 15 to 20 minutes. Remove the pipes from the refrigerator. Spoon 2 tablespoons of the remaining chocolate into the bottom of each pipe, being careful not to break the hardened latticed chocolate. Spread the chocolate evenly with the back of a spoon. Refrigerate until needed.

continued

MAKE THE CHOCOLATE PISTACHIO MOUSSE:

6. Weigh out 7 ounces of the semisweet chocolate and melt with the unsweetened chocolate in the top of a double boiler or in a medium glass bowl in a microwave oven (see Techniques, page 191), and stir until smooth.

7. Place the cream in the bowl of a stand electric mixer fitted with a balloon whip. Whisk on high until peaks form, about 1½ minutes.

8. Whisk the egg whites in the clean bowl of a stand electric mixer fitted with a clean balloon whip on high until stiff peaks form, about 2 minutes. (The bowl and whip need to be meticulously clean and dry; otherwise the egg whites will not whisk properly.)

9. Add about 1 cup of the whipped cream to the melted chocolate and whisk quickly, vigorously, and thoroughly. Add this to the egg whites, and then add the remaining whipped cream. Use a rubber spatula to fold all together gently but thoroughly. Fold in ¾ cup of the pistachios (save the rest for garnish) and the remaining 3 ounces of chocolate. Refrigerate the mousse.

ASSEMBLE THE REFUGES AND SERVE:

10. Remove the PVC pipes from the refrigerator. Fit a pastry bag with a large star tip and fill it with the mousse. Pipe the mousse into each chocolate cylinder, filling each to the edge of the chocolate-latticed paper. Sprinkle the top of the mousse with the reserved pistachios. Refrigerate for at least 1 hour before serving.

11. Remove the Refuges from the refrigerator. Slip the PVC pipe up and away from each Refuge. Carefully peel away the parchment paper. If the chocolate sticks, use a paring knife to help separate the chocolate shell from the paper. Serve immediately, accompanied by White Chocolate Spiced Rum Sauce.

THE CHEF'S TOUCH

We purchase PVC (polyvinyl chloride) pipe sections at our local Ace hardware store. They cut sections to our specifications.

I do not recommend using preshelled pistachios, because I find their mealy texture unacceptable. For this recipe purchase 2 cups of pistachios in the shell; this should yield 1 cup of shelled nuts. After shelling the nuts, drop them into boiling water for 3 minutes, then drain in a colander. Place the drained pistachios in the center of a dry cotton towel, then fold the towel over the nuts and rub vigorously to remove the skins. Now toast the nuts (see Techniques, page 192).

Once assembled, this dessert is best served within 24 hours.

chocolate orange cheesecake SERVES 10 TO 12

Commingling chocolate with orange flavor may seem odd, unless you were lucky enough to get chocolate orange candies in your Christmas stocking, like I did. Brittle chocolate on the outside, with a softer chocolate-orange interior, these candies were my favorite. Chocolate orange cheesecake conjures up—and even surpasses—those fond memories (these days I prefer a silk tie in my stocking!).

CHOCOLATE CHIP MACADAMIA NUT COOKIE CRUST

6 just-baked Chocolate Chip Macadamia Nut Cookies (see page 72)

3 tablespoons unsalted butter, melted

CHOCOLATE ORANGE CHEESECAKE FILLINGS

9 ounces semisweet baking chocolate, coarsely chopped

¾ cup heavy cream

Four 8-ounce packages cream cheese, softened

1 cup granulated sugar

1 teaspoon salt

4 large eggs

1 teaspoon pure orange extract

2 tablespoons orange juice

1 tablespoon thin julienne orange zest

CHOCOLATE GANACHE AND GARNISH

6 ounces semisweet baking chocolate, coarsely chopped

⅔ cup heavy cream

2 tablespoons unsalted butter

2 tablespoons granulated sugar

10 to 12 whole segments of mandarin oranges, drained

MAKE THE CHOCOLATE CHIP MACADAMIA NUT COOKIE CRUST:

1. After baking the cookies, leave the oven turned on to 300°F. Coat a 9 × 3–inch springform pan with the melted butter.

2. Place the still-warm cookies on the bottom of the pan, and use your fingers to press down on the cookies to form a uniformly thick surface. Bake the cookie crust for 5 minutes. Remove from the oven and leave the oven on.

MAKE THE CHOCOLATE ORANGE CHEESECAKE FILLINGS:

3. Place a 13 × 9 × 2–inch baking pan on the bottom rack of the oven. Pour 4 cups water into the pan. Close the oven door! (This allows the steam—needed for the cheesecake's velvety texture—to develop.)

4. Melt the chocolate in the cream in the top of a double boiler or in a medium glass bowl in a microwave oven (see Techniques, page 191), and stir until smooth.

continued

5. Place the cream cheese, sugar, and salt in the bowl of a stand electric mixer fitted with a paddle. Beat on low for 1 minute, on medium for 1 minute, then on high for 1 minute. Stop and scrape down the sides of the bowl and the paddle, and return to high for 1 minute more. The mixture should be very soft. Scrape down again. Add the eggs 2 at a time, beating on medium for 15 seconds after each addition, and scrape down again once all of the eggs have been incorporated. Add the orange extract and beat on medium for 15 seconds. Remove the bowl from the mixer. Use a rubber spatula to finish mixing the batter until it is smooth and thoroughly combined. Pour half of the batter into a large bowl. Add the orange juice and zest, and use a rubber spatula to fold them in until combined. Add the melted chocolate to the remaining half of the batter in the mixer bowl, and fold together until thoroughly combined.

6. Pour the chocolate cheesecake filling into the prepared springform pan. Slowly pour the orange cheesecake filling over the chocolate filling. Marbleize the batter by dipping a spoon or the flat blade of a dinner knife into the batters, without touching the bottom, and then lifting the bowl of the spoon or the blade of the knife out of the batters in a folding motion, like the roll of a wave; repeat about 24 times, working around the entire pan.

7. Cover the top of the pan with aluminum foil and bake on the center rack of the oven. Remove the foil after 1½ hours, and bake until the filling reaches 170°F, about 45 minutes more. Use a digital thermometer (see Equipment, page 186) for an accurate reading. Remove the cheesecake from the oven, and cool at room temperature for 1 hour. Refrigerate the cheesecake for 12 hours before making the ganache (do not remove from the springform pan).

MAKE THE CHOCOLATE GANACHE AND GARNISH:

8. Place the chocolate in a medium heatproof bowl. Bring the cream, butter, and sugar to a boil in a small saucepan over medium heat, stirring to dissolve the sugar. Pour the cream over the chocolate; stir with a whisk until smooth. Cover the top of the bowl with plastic wrap and refrigerate until 1 hour before decorating the cheesecake.

9. To release the cheesecake from the springform pan, wrap a damp, hot towel around the sides of the pan. Make sure the towel covers the sides completely. Hold the towel around the pan for about 1 minute, then carefully release and remove the springform sides. If the top edge of the cheesecake is not level, trim it with a serrated knife.

10. Fit a pastry bag with a large star tip and fill the bag with the room-temperature ganache. Pipe out a circle of stars (about 2 inches high and ½ inch wide), each one touching the next, along the outside edge of the top of the cheesecake. Garnish the top of the stars with the desired amount of mandarin orange segments. (Are you going to make 10 or 12 people very happy?)

11. Heat the blade of a serrated knife under hot running water and wipe dry before cutting each slice.

THE CHEF'S TOUCH

The cream cheese may be quickly softened by unwrapping it and placing it in the microwave for about 30 seconds.

For the julienne orange zest, use a sharp vegetable peeler to remove just the colored part of the skin, not the bitter white pith under the skin. Once you have removed the colored skin, use a very sharp cook's knife to cut the skin into as thin slivers as possible.

An 11-ounce can of mandarin oranges contains about 16 segments. If fresh tangerines are available, that's even better, but be sure to seed them and remove them from the membranes. After assembly, you may keep the cheesecake in the refrigerator for 2 to 3 days before serving. To prevent the cheesecake from absorbing refrigerator odors, store it in a tightly sealed plastic container.

santa's workshop

almond cookies

MAKES EIGHTEEN 4-INCH COOKIES

Delicate Almond Cookies make an appearance in this book as the texture in Chocolate Almond Cookie Bark (see Been Nice Sweets, page 79). The good news is that only 6 cookies are needed for the bark. So what to do with the remaining dozen? Oh, let's see—very pleasing with a cup of tea and quite delightful with a mug of hot chocolate. I think you get my drift, and it does not need to be shoveled!

Vegetable pan spray

1 cup granulated sugar

¾ cup all-purpose flour

6 large egg whites (⅔ cup)

4 tablespoons (½ stick) unsalted butter, melted

¼ teaspoon almond extract

1¾ cups sliced almonds, toasted (see Techniques, page 192)

1. Preheat the oven to 300°F.

2. Line 2 baking sheets with sides with parchment paper. Lightly spray the parchment on each baking sheet with vegetable pan spray.

3. Combine the sugar and flour in a large bowl, and stir with a rubber spatula until thoroughly combined. Add the egg whites, butter, and almond extract, and mix until thoroughly combined and smooth. Add 1½ cups of the almonds, and stir gently until combined.

4. Using 1 heaping tablespoon or 1 level #50 ice-cream scoop, portion 4 cookies on each baking sheet, 3 inches apart widthwise and lengthwise. Moving quickly, use an icing spatula to evenly spread the batter into a circle approximately 4 inches in diameter. Sprinkle about 1½ teaspoons of the remaining toasted almonds onto each circle of batter. Bake on the top and center racks of the oven for 25 minutes, until uniformly light golden brown. (Switch the sheets between top and center and rotate each sheet 180 degrees halfway through the baking time.)

5. Immediately invert the parchment paper onto a cooling rack. Release the cookies by pulling the parchment paper away from the cookies. Cool the cookies to room temperature on the cooling rack. Line the baking sheets with new paper.

6. Repeat the baking process with the remaining batter until all the cookies have been baked. Store the cookies at room temperature in a tightly sealed plastic container.

THE CHEF'S TOUCH

Almond Cookies will keep for several days at room temperature if stored in a tightly sealed plastic container. Due to the delicate nature of this cookie, I do not recommend freezing them, nor do I recommend shipping. If you are inclined to hand deliver (as a much appreciated gift), place small sheets of parchment or wax paper in between each cookie.

cranberry marmalade

MAKES 2 CUPS

Throw out the cans of cranberry sauce, Mama, and bring this marmalade to the table to dance with either the sweets or the turkey.

4 cups fresh or frozen whole cranberries

¼ cup granulated sugar

¼ cup orange juice

1½ teaspoons freshly grated orange zest

1 cinnamon stick

1 cup pecans, toasted (see Techniques, page 192) and coarsely chopped

1. Combine the cranberries, sugar, orange juice, zest, and cinnamon stick in a medium saucepan over medium heat and stir to dissolve the sugar. Bring to a boil, then adjust the heat so the mixture simmers. Cook until the cranberries burst and the mixture has thickened, about 5 minutes.

2. Remove from the heat and discard the cinnamon stick. Transfer the marmalade to a nonreactive container with a tightly fitting lid, and cool in the refrigerator without the lid. Once the marmalade is chilled, fold in the chopped pecans, then securely cover the container. Keep refrigerated.

THE CHEF'S TOUCH

All berries seem to have a love affair with chocolate. Even cranberries' relationship with chocolate is harmonious in our marmalade because the piquant berries are mated with the perfect amount of sugar and citrus. It's sweet enough to be pleasant with toast, but couples beautifully with several recipes in this book.

The marmalade will keep for up to 2 weeks refrigerated in a nonreactive container with a tightly fitting lid.

cranberry "punch" sorbet

MAKES 1¾ QUARTS

Even if it's cold outside, you'll still enjoy this spirited sorbet. It's like Christmas punch frozen until it sparkles. The bourbon and wine give the sorbet a distinct flavor that's perfect for a celebration. 'Tis the season to be jolly (but remember that the alcohol burns off during the cooking process).

6 cups fresh or frozen whole cranberries

2 cups granulated sugar

2 cups dry white wine

½ cup bourbon

1 tablespoon freshly grated orange zest

1½ teaspoons freshly grated lemon zest

1. Combine all of the ingredients with 2 cups water in a large saucepan over high heat, stirring to dissolve the sugar. Bring to a boil, then reduce the heat and simmer, covered, until all of the cranberries burst, about 10 minutes. Strain the liquid from the cranberry pulp through a fine-gauge strainer into a medium bowl (discard the pulp).

2. Fill the sink or a large bowl with ice and water. Place the medium bowl in the ice-water bath, and cool the liquid to a temperature of 40° to 45°F. Freeze in an ice-cream machine following the manufacturer's instructions.

3. Transfer the sorbet to a 2-quart plastic container. Securely cover the container, then place in the freezer for several hours before serving.

THE CHEF'S TOUCH

Dreaming about the combination of a warm Chocolate Fruitycake (see Home for the Holidays, page 2) and ice cold Cranberry "Punch" Sorbet is enough to have me wishing it was the holidays all year round.

This sorbet is at its best when served within 4 days of preparation. Keep the container of sorbet securely covered in the freezer to prevent the sorbet from dehydrating and absorbing freezer odors.

sweet and sour sugar cookies

MAKES THIRTY-SIX 3-INCH COOKIES

This cookie will woo your senses. It looks and smells like your soon-to-be favorite holiday memory, and it melts in your mouth like an early snow.

3¼ cups all-purpose flour

¼ teaspoon baking soda

¼ teaspoon salt

10 tablespoons (1¼ sticks) unsalted butter, softened

1 cup granulated sugar

1 large egg

1 tablespoon plus 1½ teaspoons dark rum

⅓ cup sour cream

3 tablespoons pearl sugar (see The Chef's Touch, page 170)

1. Preheat the oven to 325°F. Line 3 baking sheets with parchment or wax paper.

2. In a sifter, combine 3 cups of the flour, the baking soda, and salt. Sift onto a large piece of parchment or wax paper.

3. Place the butter and sugar in the bowl of a stand electric mixer fitted with a paddle. Mix on low for 1 minute, then on medium for 1 minute, then on high for 1 minute. Stop and scrape down the sides of the bowl, and beat for 1 minute more on high. Scrape down again, add the egg and rum, and mix on medium for 1 minute until incorporated. Scrape down again. Turn the mixer on to low and gradually add the dry ingredients; mix until incorporated, about 2 minutes, and scrape down again. Add the sour cream and mix on low until all the dough pulls away from the sides of the bowl, about 30 seconds. Remove the bowl from the mixer.

4. Lightly flour a clean, dry work surface with some of the remaining ¼ cup flour. Transfer the dough to the work surface and knead gently to form a smooth ball. Wrap the dough in plastic wrap and refrigerate for 30 minutes.

continued

5. Remove the dough from the refrigerator, and remove and discard the plastic wrap. If necessary, reflour the work surface. Place the dough on the work surface, and shape into a log 18 inches long and 1 inch high (use the remaining flour as necessary to prevent sticking).

6. Cut the log into thirty-six ½-inch-thick slices. Divide the slices, evenly spaced, onto the baking sheets, laying them cut side down. Sprinkle ¼ teaspoon of pearl sugar over the top of each cookie. Place the baking sheets on the top and center racks of the oven and bake for 14 to 15 minutes, switching the sheets between top and center and rotating each sheet 180 degrees halfway through the baking time. Remove the cookies from the oven, and cool to room temperature on the baking sheets. Repeat with the remaining cookie dough, as necessary, once the baking sheets cool (hold the dough at room temperature). Store the cooled cookies in a tightly sealed plastic container.

THE CHEF'S TOUCH

Pearl sugar is a large crystal sugar that does not lose its shape during baking. It also gives the cookies that holiday look. If you are not able to locate pearl sugar at the supermarket, try www.chefshop.com (a great specialty food site).

For a vibrant cherry-flavored option, add ½ cup chopped maraschino cherries and 1 tablespoon maraschino cherry juice at the same time as the sour cream. Looks good like a holiday cookie should.

Sweet and Sour Sugar Cookies will keep for several days at room temperature when stored in a tightly sealed plastic container. For long-term storage (up to several weeks), the cookies may be frozen. Freeze in a tightly sealed plastic container to prevent them from dehydrating and absorbing freezer odors.

"sloshed santa" sauce

MAKES 4 CUPS

Mrs. Claus, please don't make this recipe until after Christmas; otherwise, Santa may be in danger of an FUI (Flying Under the Influence, with reindeer). Just kidding . . . only 2 tablespoons of active spirits are in 4 cups of sauce (the rest of the alcohol is reduced to nonintoxicating vapors). Santa—and almost any adult—could drive a sleigh worry-free after enjoying "Sloshed Santa" Sauce on a favorite confection.

⅔ cup plus 2 tablespoons Scotch, bourbon, or brandy

½ cup raisins

1¼ cups heavy cream

2 tablespoons confectioners' sugar, sifted

½ cup walnut halves, toasted (see Techniques, page 192) and chopped (preferably by hand) into ¼-inch pieces

1. Bring ⅔ cup of the chosen booze and the raisins to a boil in a small saucepan over medium heat, stirring occasionally. Reduce the heat to low and simmer, stirring occasionally, until almost all of the liquor has been absorbed by the raisins or has evaporated, 7 to 8 minutes. Transfer the sloshed raisins to a dinner plate, spreading evenly. Refrigerate until needed.

2. Place the cream, confectioners' sugar, and the remaining 2 tablespoons of spirits in the bowl of a stand electric mixer fitted with a balloon whip. Whisk the mixture on medium-high until very soft peaks form, about 1 minute; the mixture should be fluffy but smooth, not stiff. Add the chilled raisins and the walnuts, and use a rubber spatula to fold them into the whipped cream. Transfer the sauce to a 2-quart plastic container. Securely cover the container and refrigerate until needed.

THE CHEF'S TOUCH

The "Sloshed Santa" Sauce is best when served within a day of preparation. Keep the sauce securely covered to prevent it from absorbing refrigerator odors.

pistachio raisin biscotti

MAKES 30 BISCOTTI

Have yourself a merry little biscotti, and if you make it a Pistachio Raisin Biscotti, you will experience an intensely crunchy cookie peppered with flavorful raisins and pistachios. *Buon appetito!*

2 cups plus 2 tablespoons all-purpose flour

1½ teaspoons baking powder

½ teaspoon salt

¾ cup granulated sugar

8 tablespoons (1 stick) unsalted butter, cut into 1-tablespoon pieces and softened

2 large eggs

1 teaspoon pure vanilla extract

½ cup shelled pistachios, skinned, toasted (see Techniques, page 192), and coarsely chopped

½ cup raisins

1. Preheat the oven to 325°F. Line a baking sheet with parchment or wax paper.

2. In a sifter, combine 2 cups flour, the baking powder, and salt. Sift onto a large piece of parchment or wax paper.

3. Place the sugar and butter in the bowl of a stand electric mixer fitted with a paddle. Mix on low for 1 minute, then on medium for 1 minute more. Stop and scrape down the sides of the bowl and the paddle, then beat on medium-high for 1 minute. Scrape down again. Add the eggs one at a time, beating on medium for 30 seconds after each addition and scraping down again once the eggs have been incorporated. Add the vanilla and beat on medium for 15 seconds. Turn the mixer to low and gradually add the dry ingredients; mix until incorporated, about 15 seconds. Scrape down again. Add the pistachios and raisins, and mix on low until incorporated, about 10 seconds.

4. Lightly flour a clean, dry work surface with some of the remaining flour. Transfer the dough to the work surface, and knead gently for several seconds to finish mixing the dough. Divide the dough into 2 equal portions, and shape each into a log 12 inches long, 1½ inches wide, and 1½ inches high. Carefully place the 2 logs, about 2 inches apart, onto the lined baking sheet. Bake on the center rack of the oven for 40 minutes (rotating the sheet 180 degrees halfway through the baking time) until lightly browned and slightly firm to the touch. Remove from the oven and reduce the oven temperature to 275°F. Cool the logs on a wire rack at room temperature for about 15 minutes. Line 2 baking sheets with clean parchment.

5. Place the logs on a cutting board. Using a sharp serrated knife, trim the rounded ends from each log. Cut each log into fifteen ¾-inch-thick diagonal slices. Lay 15 slices flat, evenly spaced, onto each of the baking sheets. Bake the biscotti slices on the top and center rack of the oven for 30 minutes until crisp and light golden brown, switching the sheets between top and center and rotating each sheet 180 degrees halfway through the baking time. Remove from the oven and transfer the biscotti to a wire rack to thoroughly cool before storing in a tightly sealed plastic container.

THE CHEF'S TOUCH

I recommend that you take the time to shell your own pistachios. Already shelled pistachios lack flavor and are soft, and neither characteristic improves, even after toasting.

The biscotti will remain crispy and delicious for 2 to 3 weeks stored at room temperature in a tightly sealed plastic container.

frangelico cream sauce

MAKES 1 CUP

Frangelico Cream Sauce is an elegant sauce imbued with the delicate flavor of hazelnuts. It will fashion desserts into haute cuisine wherever or whenever this rich, nutty flavor is desired.

1½ teaspoons cornstarch

1 cup heavy cream

3 tablespoons Frangelico liqueur

2 tablespoons granulated sugar

½ teaspoon pure vanilla extract

1. Whisk together the cornstarch and 1 teaspoon water in a small bowl until the corn starch is dissolved and the mixture is smooth.

2. Bring the cream, Frangelico, and sugar to a boil in a small saucepan over medium-high heat, stirring to dissolve the sugar. Remove from the heat, whisk in the dissolved cornstarch, and continue to whisk until the sauce thickens slightly, about 45 seconds. Cool in an ice-water bath to 40° to 45°F. Add the vanilla extract and whisk gently to combine. Refrigerate in a tightly sealed plastic container.

THE CHEF'S TOUCH

Depending on the dessert collaboration, many other liqueurs can be substituted in the same proportion in this sauce. You are the bartender, so consider Godiva liqueur, amaretto, even green crème de menthe, or my favorite, sambuca.

The Frangelico Cream Sauce will keep for up to 3 days stored in a tightly sealed plastic container in the refrigerator.

butterscotch sauce

MAKES 1½ CUPS

Spiked with Buttershots Schnapps, our butterscotch sauce has a suave, lavish flavor and a smooth texture that will enhance any confection. The first taste made me a kid again, when butterscotch came only in the form of candy.

1 cup tightly packed dark brown sugar

1 cup heavy cream

1 tablespoon plus 1½ teaspoons Buttershots Schnapps

1. Bring the sugar and ¼ cup water to a boil in a medium saucepan over medium heat, stirring frequently to dissolve the sugar. Continue to boil until it reaches 240°F, about 4 minutes. Use a digital thermometer (see Equipment, page 186) for an accurate reading. Remove from the heat.

2. Bring the cream to a boil in a small saucepan over medium-high heat. Gradually and carefully pour the hot cream into the hot sugar and mix with a long-handled whisk until the cream is incorporated. Once all of the cream has been incorporated, cool the sauce in an ice-water bath to 40° to 45°F.

3. Whisk the Buttershots Schnapps into the cold sauce. Refrigerate the sauce in a tightly sealed plastic container.

THE CHEF'S TOUCH

Butterscotch sauce typically contains butter. We chose to use heavy cream rather than butter in our sauce, with excellent butterscotchy results.

Buttershots Schnapps, made from a rum base enhanced with butterscotch flavor, is widely available. If, however, you are not able to locate it, you may substitute a butterscotch liqueur. You may also eliminate it from the recipe if you choose, and you will still have a pretty good sauce.

Butterscotch Sauce will keep for up to a week stored in a tightly sealed plastic container in the refrigerator.

grasshopper chocolate chunk cookies

MAKES TWENTY-FOUR 3-INCH COOKIES

Green crème de menthe and chocolate chunks will have this cookie hopping into your mouth with ease. Include the suggested chocolate drizzle and the cookies will be gone in the wink of an eye.

2 cups all-purpose flour

1 cup confectioners' sugar

10 tablespoons (1¼ sticks) cold unsalted butter, cut into ½-tablespoon pieces

3 large egg yolks

1 tablespoon green crème de menthe

1 teaspoon pure vanilla extract

4 ounces semisweet baking chocolate, coarsely chopped

¼ cup granulated sugar

1. Preheat the oven to 350°F. Line 3 baking sheets with parchment or wax paper.

2. Place 1¾ cups of the flour and the confectioners' sugar in the bowl of a stand electric mixer fitted with a paddle. Mix on low for 10 seconds to blend.

3. Add the cold butter (it needs to be cold for the dough to work properly), one piece at a time, while mixing on low, until the mixture is mealy in texture, about 2 minutes. Add the egg yolks, green crème de menthe, and vanilla, and then mix on low until the ingredients start to form a dough, about 30 seconds. Add the chocolate, and mix on low for 15 seconds to combine.

4. Lightly flour a clean, dry work surface with some of the remaining ¼ cup flour. Transfer the dough to the work surface and knead gently to finish incorporating the chocolate. Shape the dough into two 12-inch-long, 1½-inch-high logs. Cut each log into twelve 1-inch-thick slices. Roll each piece of dough into a smooth, round ball, then flatten each ball in the palm of your hand into a circle 2¾ to 3 inches in diameter.

5. Place the granulated sugar in a small bowl. Press one flat side of each dough circle into the granulated sugar to lightly coat, then place 8 pieces of dough, sugar side up, evenly spaced, onto each of the 3 prepared baking sheets. Bake on the top and center racks in the preheated oven for 6 minutes (that's correct—just 6 minutes), until lightly golden brown around the edges. Remove the cookies from the oven, and cool at room temperature on the baking sheets for 20 minutes. Repeat with the remaining cookie dough, as necessary, once the baking sheets cool (hold the dough at room temperature). Once cool, the cookies may be stored in a tightly sealed plastic container.

THE CHEF'S TOUCH

You can elevate the chocolate factor by drizzling melted chocolate over the cooled cookies. About 4 ounces semisweet baking chocolate should do the trick.

A pert peppermint twist for the cookie would be to replace the chocolate in the recipe with 4 ounces crushed peppermint candy canes.

Grasshopper Chocolate Chunk Cookies will stay fresh in a tightly sealed plastic container at room temperature for 2 to 3 days or in the refrigerator for a week to 10 days (bring the cookies to room temperature before eating). The cookies may also be frozen in a tightly sealed plastic container for several weeks. Thaw the frozen cookies at room temperature before serving.

miss junie mae's peanut brittle

MAKES SLIGHTLY MORE THAN 1½ POUNDS

Ding Dong! Merrily on High.
Miss Junie Mae's Peanut Brittle is the best, don't deny.

Odd to say that a recipe without chocolate would be worthy of this book, but Miss Junie Mae's brittle is so exceptional that I wouldn't go to press without it.

Vegetable pan spray

1½ cups granulated sugar

¾ cup dark corn syrup

2 cups unsalted roasted peanuts, skinned

2 teaspoons baking soda

1. Lightly spray a baking sheet with sides with vegetable pan spray.

2. Combine the sugar and corn syrup in a large saucepan over medium-high heat. When the mixture is hot (about 140°F), stir with a long-handled metal spoon to combine. Bring to a boil, 1½ to 2 minutes. Reduce the heat to medium and stir occasionally until it reaches 330°F, about 6½ minutes. Use a digital thermometer (see Equipment, page 186) for an accurate reading. Remove from the heat.

3. Working quickly and carefully, as the mixture is extremely hot, add the peanuts and stir with the long-handled metal spoon to combine. Add the baking soda and stir until incorporated.

4. Carefully pour this mixture onto the prepared baking sheet and allow the mixture to spread out on its own. Cool at room temperature for 45 to 60 minutes, until hard. Break the brittle by hand into pieces. Store at room temperature in a tightly sealed plastic container.

THE CHEF'S TOUCH

Every Christmas for the last several years, I have been the recipient of a large tin of the most remarkably delicious peanut brittle I have ever eaten, thanks to the kindness of Ann and Lew Carr of Suffolk, Virginia, frequent patrons of the Trellis.

The Carr's agreed to share this exceptional recipe, but they insisted that their hometown brittle-making legend Miss Junie Mae get the credit. Miss Junie Mae, who lived in the farming community of Isle of Wight County, Virginia, shared her recipe for peanut brittle with countless people in the community including Ann's mother, who years later passed it on to Ann. Ann and Lew take turns preparing the brittle every holiday season because they make so much of it!

The brittle can be stored for 2 to 3 weeks at room temperature in a tightly sealed plastic container. (I cannot possibly imagine that it would not be eaten sooner.) You may also freeze the brittle, but be sure to thaw it before attempting a taste.

peanut butter berry sauce

MAKES 1¼ CUPS

Wilderberry® Schnapps gives this sauce an adult nuance. But don't be cruel; even the kids can indulge without your worrying that they will be rocking around the Christmas tree.

¾ tablespoon cornstarch

½ cup plus 2 tablespoons heavy cream

¼ cup half-and-half

¼ cup creamy peanut butter, melted (see The Chef's Touch, below)

2 tablespoons granulated sugar

1 tablespoon plus 1½ teaspoons DeKuyper Wilderberry Schnapps

1. Whisk together the cornstarch and ½ teaspoon water in a small bowl until the cornstarch is dissolved and the mixture is smooth.

2. Bring the heavy cream, half-and-half, peanut butter, and sugar to a boil in a small saucepan over medium heat, stirring to dissolve the sugar. Remove from the heat. Whisk in the dissolved cornstarch, then return to medium heat and continue to whisk until the sauce thickens slightly, 15 to 20 seconds. Remove from the heat and transfer to a small heatproof bowl. Whisk in the schnapps, then cool in an ice-water bath to a temperature of 40° to 45°F.

3. Once the sauce is cold, transfer it to the bowl of a food processor fitted with a metal blade. Process the sauce for 30 seconds until ever-so-smooth! Refrigerate in a tightly sealed plastic container.

THE CHEF'S TOUCH

For the melted peanut butter: Place the peanut butter into a 1-cup heatproof glass measuring cup, and microwave it for approximately 20 seconds (times will vary depending upon the wattage and power settings on your microwave oven).

Peanut Butter Berry Sauce will keep for up to a week stored in a tightly sealed plastic container in the refrigerator.

pumpkin spice crème anglaise

MAKES 1½ CUPS

Pumpkin farmers beware! Once the recipe for this splendid sauce is published, the pumpkin fields are certain to be besieged. Just the right amount of spice gives the pumpkin a spunky flavor, and the creaminess adds a dollop of class. The overall effect is downright divine.

¾ cup heavy cream

½ cup half-and-half

¼ cup granulated sugar

2 large egg yolks

¾ teaspoon cornstarch

¼ cup solid-pack pumpkin

¾ teaspoon pure vanilla extract

Pinch of ground cinnamon

Pinch of ground nutmeg

1. Bring the heavy cream, half-and-half, and 2 tablespoons of the sugar to a boil in a medium saucepan over medium heat, stirring to dissolve the sugar. Remove from the heat.

2. Place the egg yolks, the remaining 2 tablespoons sugar, and the cornstarch in a medium heatproof bowl. Whisk until thoroughly combined. Ladle ¼ cup of the hot cream into the yolks and whisk vigorously to combine. Pour this back into the saucepan and blend with a whisk. Return the saucepan to the heat, and cook on medium until it reaches 185°F. Use a digital thermometer (see Equipment, page 186) for an accurate reading.

3. Pour the mixture through a fine-gauge strainer into a medium bowl. Add the pumpkin, vanilla, cinnamon, and nutmeg, and whisk until thoroughly combined. Cool in an ice-water bath to 40° to 45°F. Refrigerate the sauce in a tightly sealed plastic container until needed.

THE CHEF'S TOUCH

The French culinary term for a light custard sauce is *crème anglaise*. Our pumpkin custard sauce may be served warm or cold.

Check the label when purchasing the canned pumpkin so that you do not purchase pumpkin pie filling rather than solid-pack pumpkin. Pumpkin pie filling is laced with spices, and as the recipe calls for spices, doubling up will overly intensify that holiday flavor.

Pumpkin Spice Crème Anglaise will keep for up to 3 days stored in a tightly sealed plastic container in the refrigerator.

vivacious vanilla ice cream

MAKES 1 QUART

Perhaps it's audacious to energize the world's favorite ice cream with vodka, but that bold move seems justified after the first spirited and creamy bite.

1½ cups heavy cream

1½ cups half-and-half

1 vanilla bean, cut in half lengthwise

4 large egg yolks

⅓ cup granulated sugar

3 tablespoons vanilla-flavored vodka

2 teaspoons pure vanilla extract

1. Bring the heavy cream, half-and-half, and vanilla bean to a boil in a medium saucepan over medium heat, then remove from the heat.

2. Place the egg yolks and sugar in a medium bowl. Whisk until thoroughly combined. Ladle ½ cup of the hot cream, 2 tablespoons at a time, into the eggs and whisk gently to incorporate.

3. Pour the egg and cream mixture back into the saucepan and whisk until thoroughly combined. Cook over medium heat, stirring constantly, until it reaches 185°F, about 1 minute. Use a digital thermometer (see Equipment, page 186) for an accurate reading. Remove from the heat.

4. Pour the mixture through a fine-gauge strainer into a large heatproof bowl. Cool in an ice-water bath to a temperature of 40° to 45°F. When the mixture is cold, add the vanilla-flavored vodka and the vanilla extract and stir gently to incorporate. Freeze in an ice-cream machine following the manufacturer's instructions.

5. Transfer the ice cream to a 2-quart plastic container. Securely cover the container, then place in the freezer for several hours before serving.

THE CHEF'S TOUCH

I am incredulous that vanilla ice cream is the whole wide world's favorite ice cream. Here in America—where we eat more ice cream per capita than anywhere else in the world—vanilla ice cream is #1 with about 30 percent of the volume consumed, and chocolate-based ice cream lags behind with only 12 percent of the volume. Go figure—but I must say that a bowl of Vivacious Vanilla is a pretty holly jolly way to go.

Vivacious Vanilla Ice Cream is best served within 5 to 6 days of preparation. Keep the container of ice cream securely covered in the freezer to prevent the ice cream from dehydrating and absorbing freezer odors.

white chocolate spiced rum sauce

MAKES 1⅓ CUPS

White chocolate and rum go together like mistletoe and kissing. This piquant sauce can dance with many partners (and don't be shy in the pairing and the portion).

4 ounces white chocolate, coarsely chopped

1 cup heavy cream

Pinch of salt

2 tablespoons spiced rum

Place the chocolate in a medium heatproof bowl. Bring the cream and salt to a boil in a small saucepan over medium heat. Pour the cream over the chocolate and stir with a whisk until smooth. Cool in an ice-water bath to 40° to 45°F. When the sauce is cold, add the rum and stir to combine. Refrigerate the sauce in a tightly sealed plastic container.

THE CHEF'S TOUCH

You may substitute your favorite rum if spiced rum is not available in your liquor cabinet, but the sprightly spice flavor will be missed.

White Chocolate Spiced Rum Sauce will keep for up to 3 days stored in a tightly sealed plastic container in the refrigerator.

equipment, ingredients, and techniques

I have listed the brands of equipment and ingredients used at Ganache Hill merely to offer a benchmark for product quality, not as an endorsement.

EQUIPMENT

I'm lucky. My test kitchen, perched on a ⅓-acre hilltop compound called Ganache Hill, is surrounded by lavish gardens. The 1,600-square-foot building that houses the test kitchen has a dining room, two offices, my collection of over 2,000 cookbooks, and lots of food-related art. However, instead of heavy-duty professional appliances and cookware, Ganache Hill is equipped like an average home kitchen.

This is important for developing and testing recipes for home bakers. Our cooktop, ovens, food processor, electric mixer, and equipment such as baking sheets and bowls were purchased from local hardware stores, supermarkets, Target, or Wal-Mart.

I recommend the following equipment for successful baking results.

BAKING SHEETS AND CAKE PANS

We use nonstick baking sheets and cake pans at Ganache Hill. Most of our baking sheets are 15 × 10 inches, and they all have sides for extra rigidity (this rigidity helps prevent the baking sheets from warping in the oven). Although the baking sheets are nonstick, we often butter and sometimes line them with parchment paper or wax paper. This ensures quick release of the baked product, be it cookie or cake. Some batters, especially those with lots of sugar, will stick even to nonstick pans. Not only will buttering and papering assist the effortless release of a product from a pan, but it also makes short work of cleanup. The following manufacturers and brands are known for quality, value, and accessibility.

EKCO Housewares: Baker's Secret

NordicWare: Bundt® Brand Bakeware

Farberware: Professional or Millennium Series

Kaiser Bakeware: Noblesse

BOWLS

Select nonreactive stainless-steel bowls as well as heatproof glass bowls, which are also nonreactive and easy to clean. Stainless-steel bowls are better heat conductors, so I suggest stainless when setting up an ice-water bath. Glass bowls are necessary for use in a microwave oven. The following bowl sizes correspond with the bowls specified in this book.

small = 1½ to 2 quarts
medium = 2½ to 3 quarts
large = 3½ to 4 quarts
extra-large = 6 to 7 quarts

DOUBLE BOILERS

At Ganache Hill, we usually nest a stainless-steel or heatproof glass bowl over a saucepan to fashion a double boiler. When using a makeshift double boiler like this, be certain the bottom half of the bowl can be inserted into the saucepan and that the bowl covers the entire top of the pan. Prior to setting the bowl over the saucepan, place about one inch of water in the pan. Don't let the bottom of the bowl touch the water. (This also applies to a real double boiler, which is comprised of two saucepans, one nesting into the other.) Keeping the bottom of the bowl or top saucepan from contact with the water will help prevent chocolate and other ingredients from getting too hot or scorching as they heat.

ELECTRIC MIXERS

At Ganache Hill we have two KitchenAid mixers, a 5-quart model K5SS and a 4½-quart K45. In my previous dessert cookbooks, almost every recipe required using a stand electric mixer. This is not the case in *I'm Dreaming of a Chocolate Christmas*. True, in order to produce the best results in many recipes, an electric mixer is necessary. To simplify some of the recipes in this book, though, I experimented with producing similar results without the aid of an electric mixer. In fact, we found that in a few instances the hand-mixed recipes were often better!

When you do use an electric mixer, I recommend you always have on hand at least one extra bowl. For example, for the White Chocolate Banana Walnut Christmas Log (see Been Naughty Sweets, page 130), after you beat the egg yolks and other ingredients for the mousse cake batter, you'll need to beat the egg whites. You'll save a lot of trouble by having an extra bowl: You can simply remove the bowl with the yolk mixture, along with the mixer paddle, and insert the extra bowl with a balloon whip for the egg whites. I also suggest purchasing a pouring shield attachment for your stand electric mixer (sometimes this useful accessory is included in the price of the mixer).

Handheld electric mixers are effective for many batters, especially if the batters are small in volume. But this type of mixer is not efficient when it comes to mixing large volumes of batter or dense dough.

ICE-CREAM MACHINES

Making ice cream at home has changed dramatically in the last few years due to innovative (hands-free and simple to use) and inexpensive machines. At one time, an electrically cooled countertop ice-cream freezer with a 2-quart capacity would set you back about $1,000. Or you could rely on a hand-cranked machine that required ice and salt and a lot of vigorous cranking.

Now you can purchase an easy-to-use electric machine that requires no cranking, ice, or salt. It freezes the ice cream in an insulated canister that is first frozen in your freezer for about 24 hours and then inserted on the electric base of the machine. With this type of machine, it takes about 30 minutes for the ice cream to freeze enough to be placed in the freezer to harden. I suggest finding a machine that makes 1½ to 2 quarts (these inexpensive machines are often available in kitchenware and department stores and even at your local Target or Wal-Mart).

ICE-CREAM SCOOPS

Ice-cream scoops are very effective for portioning batters into muffin tins and for portioning cookie dough. Scooping batter or dough is much quicker than using a tablespoon measure. Scoops are available in a variety of sizes from a large #12 (3-ounce) scoop to a small #70 (½-ounce) scoop. The number, found on the bottom of the handle or inside the scoop itself, refers to the approximate number of scoops per quart.

MICROWAVE OVENS

For melting chocolate, my preference is a microwave oven (see Techniques, page 191) rather than a double boiler. It is simpler and quicker, and also I find that less chocolate is wasted due to error.

The settings vary widely on microwave ovens from different manufacturers, so I urge caution when following explicit directions. Be on the safe side and initially err in favor of caution by microwaving the chocolate, or whatever else you are heating, on a lower setting and for less time than listed in the instructions.

PARCHMENT AND WAX PAPERS

Lining baking sheets or cake pans with parchment or wax paper helps to ensure that cookies do not stick to the baking sheets and cake layers release effortlessly from the pans. Although lining pans is not always necessary, when it is specified in this cookbook, it's because we found it was particularly helpful. Parchment paper can stand exposure to high baking temperatures, and in some cases can be reused. Wax paper is not reusable. In most situations in this book, wax paper may be used as a substitute for parchment.

PASTRY BAGS

Forget about traditional canvas pastry bags or plastic-lined fabric pastry bags. I find cleaning and drying these bags tedious. Disposable plastic pastry bags are the way to go—simply pipe and then discard. Check out kitchenware stores or www.wilton.com for disposable decorating bags. In a pinch, a resealable plastic bag will work.

SPATULAS

OFFSET SPATULA I have found that a spatula with an offset blade is very handy for spreading batter inside cake pans. Although a rubber spatula or a straight icing spatula could be used, the offset spatula does a better job of spreading within the confines of a cake pan. I recommend an offset spatula with a 4- to 5-inch-long, ¾-inch-wide blade.

RUBBER SPATULA The rubber spatula is one of the most effective tools a baker or cook can have in the equipment drawer. No other tool is as useful for removing every last ounce of batter, chocolate, or other food from inside a receptacle. I recommend an extensive collection of all sizes of rubber spatulas, as well as a few heat-resistant silicone spatulas for working with very hot ingredients.

UTILITY TURNER A utility turner, which is a wide offset spatula with a blade about 3 inches wide and 7 to 8 inches long, is useful for transferring a cake layer from a cardboard cake circle to a serving platter as well as for other situations where size makes the difference.

THERMOMETERS

DIGITAL THERMOMETER For many years I used a Taylor brand glass candy thermometer with a range of 100° to 400°F, housed in a stainless-steel jacket, to accurately measure the temperature of bubbling hot sugar or frying oil. I have now moved into the twenty-first century since I was introduced to the Pyrex® Professional™ Digital Thermometer with a commercial quality stainless-steel probe. This fairly inexpensive thermometer is simple to use, gives precise temperature readings, and even has a timer. This thermometer has also replaced the instant-read thermometer I used to recommend. Search the Web for online sources.

OVEN THERMOMETER The only way to ensure that your oven is operating at a designated temperature is to place a mercury-filled tube thermometer in the oven and adjust the heat according to the thermometer, rather than rely on the oven setting. This type of thermometer may be left in the oven at all times. The only exception is during the self-clean operation, which produces high enough heat to ruin most thermometers. The Taylor Commercial Oven Guide Thermometer is available online from www.target.com and other Web sites.

WHISKS

A whisk is a hands-on piece of equipment essential for many kitchen procedures. I suggest a few different sizes of stainless-steel whisks from 6 to 12 inches in length, equally divided between light, flexible whisks (for light batters, whipped cream, and meringues) and heavier gauge, sturdy whisks (for sauces, heavily textured batters, and ganache).

INGREDIENTS

Although I own a restaurant (the Trellis in Williamsburg, Virginia) and have access to food-service products, all of the ingredients needed for testing the recipes in this cookbook were purchased in our local supermarkets. We wanted to be sure to use the same ingredients that you would.

Quality ingredients are the key to successful baking. A baker should never settle for anything other than first-rate ingredients. For that reason, I recommend that you buy the ingredients as close to the time of preparation as possible. Even shelf-stable products such as baking soda, spices, chocolate, and unsweetened cocoa powder will deteriorate if stored in the cupboard for too long, so purchase small containers. Bulk quantities may seem more economical, but unless you plan on baking for the masses, shopping for only the quantities you need will help ensure quality baked goods.

Read the list of ingredients in the recipe before you start, and make sure you have all the ingredients on hand. Organize the ingredients as listed in the recipe, which means cut the butter into 1-tablespoon pieces, chop the chocolate, measure the flour, and so on, and don't start production until you have all the ingredients assembled and ready as described.

You can use the following information about some of the key ingredients used throughout this cookbook as a guide to selecting the specific quality of product you need to prepare extraordinary desserts.

BAKING SODA AND BAKING POWDER

Baking soda (which is pure bicarbonate of soda) needs to combine with an acidic ingredient like buttermilk to start leavening, while baking powder (which is an amalgam of bicarbonate of soda, cream of tartar, and cornstarch) starts leavening no matter what the liquid, as the cream of tartar it contains provides the acidity. I should also note that as soon as the soda or powder is added to a batter, leavening begins. So don't waste time completing the batter and getting it into the oven.

Always check the expiration date on the package. Outdated leavening may not work—especially baking powder. Be precise in the measurement of either of these ingredients, as too much or too little will not deliver the desired results.

At Ganache Hill we use Calumet brand baking powder and Arm & Hammer baking soda.

BUTTER

Butter contributes positively on all fronts to baked desserts and unbaked confections such as ganache. In baked desserts, butter enhances flavor, moistness, crumb texture, and even leavening. With ganache, candies, and other unbaked sweets, butter imparts a sensual pleasure to the palate that makes goodies so gratifying.

At Ganache Hill we bake and cook with Land O'Lakes brand U.S. Grade AA unsalted butter. Butter should be stored in the refrigerator or the freezer to deter rancidity. Many of our recipes call for softened butter, but remember that unsalted butter should never remain at room temperature for more than a few hours; it will soften within two to three hours.

For long-term storage (more than a week), I suggest storing butter in the freezer. Always thaw frozen butter in the refrigerator rather than at room temperature (this may take a couple of days).

If you are not able to purchase unsalted butter, you may use salted butter for the recipes in this book without altering the recipes.

CHOCOLATE

PURCHASING CHOCOLATE Be sure to read the ingredient list on the package to verify that you are purchasing real chocolate. If the label lists any fat other than cocoa butter, it's not the real thing. Some manufacturers add palm kernel oil or coconut oil, which rob the chocolate of the voluptuous mouthfeel derived from cocoa butter.

STORING CHOCOLATE Store chocolate in a cool and dry place, at a temperature range of 65° to 68°F with 50 percent relative humidity. Air-conditioned room temperature in the range of 68° to 78°F also works fine. If storage conditions are too warm, the chocolate may develop gray surface streaks caused by the cocoa butter rising to the surface. When conditions are damp, the sugar may also rise to the surface. Chocolate so affected is safe to eat, but I do not recommend using it for baking. Due to its unstable condition it can give less than desirable results. I recommend buying only the amount of chocolate you need for a particular recipe to avoid worrying about storage conditions.

types of chocolate

Chocolate Chips and Mini Morsels Most chips and morsels are formulated differently from baking chocolate, which is the reason they maintain their shape even after being baked. As with other chocolate, choose only chips and mini morsels that have cocoa butter as the only fat, not palm or coconut oil. At Ganache Hill we use Baker's® semi-sweet real chocolate chips and Nestlé Toll House Semi-Sweet Chocolate Mini Morsels.

Semisweet Baking Chocolate Semisweet baking chocolate is comprised of unsweetened chocolate (a minimum of 35 percent by law), cocoa butter, sugar, soy lecithin (an emulsifier that keeps the chocolate smooth and liquid), and vanilla extract. Many of the recipes in this book contain some amount of semisweet baking chocolate. If you prefer darker, more assertively flavored chocolate, you may substitute bittersweet chocolate (which contains a higher percentage of unsweetened chocolate than semisweet) in exactly the same amount in any of our recipes. As mentioned previously, do not purchase chocolate that contains any fat other than cocoa butter. At Ganache Hill, we use Baker's Semi-Sweet Baking Chocolate Squares.

Never substitute chocolate chips or chocolate mini morsels in recipes calling for semisweet baking chocolate. Although pleasing to eat from the bag and deliciously textural in cookies and countless other recipes, chips and mini morsels are not suitable substitutes for baking chocolate.

Unsweetened Baking Chocolate Unsweetened baking chocolate, sometimes called chocolate liquor, is the juice produced when roasted cocoa beans are ground and processed into liquid. After additional processing to ensure smoothness, the liquid is hardened into blocks. The package labeling for unsweetened chocolate should list one ingredient: chocolate. Unsweetened chocolate is not eaten on its own, but it is the core of other baking chocolates such as semisweet chocolate. Unsweetened chocolate is composed of more than 50 percent cocoa butter, with the rest cocoa solids. It contains no sugar or other additives. At Ganache Hill, we use Baker's Unsweetened Baking Chocolate Squares.

Unsweetened Cocoa Powder The intense chocolate flavor that is achieved in a recipe by using unsweetened cocoa powder is due to the low fat content of the cocoa. Cocoa is produced by hydraulically pressing unsweetened chocolate (which contains 50 to 56 percent cocoa butter) in order to remove most of the cocoa butter. Cocoa, however, is not totally fat free; it does contain residual amounts of cocoa butter.

The lack of cocoa butter makes cocoa highly soluble in liquid—think hot chocolate. The flavor intensity of cocoa is diminished by exposure to air, so I recommend purchasing small containers and keeping the container tightly sealed. Look at the container closely before purchasing to make certain you are not selecting a cocoa drink mix. The only ingredient listed on the package should be cocoa. At Ganache Hill, we use Natural Hershey's Cocoa (not Dutch process).

White Chocolate The ingredient list on a package of white chocolate should include only sugar, cocoa butter, milk, soy lecithin, and vanilla extract. It is important to check the package of white chocolate before purchasing; you will not want to purchase it if palm kernel oil or coconut oil are listed. At Ganache Hill, we use Baker's Premium White Chocolate Baking Squares.

CREAM

All of the recipes in this cookbook were tested using ultra-pasteurized cream we purchased at the supermarket. One big advantage that ultra-pasteurized cream has over fresh cream is a significant shelf life; it will stay "fresh" under refrigeration for weeks. On the slight downside, ultra-pasteurized cream does not burst with pure flavor as fresh cream does. When used as an ingredient, though, ultra-pasteurized cream is almost impossible to differentiate from fresh cream when eating a dessert. At Ganache Hill, we used Richfood® Heavy Whipping Cream. You can also use whatever brand is available in your local market.

EGGS

Fresh Grade AA large eggs are essential for the success of the recipes in this cookbook. Always purchase eggs from a refrigerated case, and get them back into refrigeration as soon as possible. Using smaller or larger size eggs may have a negative impact on many recipes in this cookbook. Although substituting one size egg for another may sometimes work, it can't be guaranteed. In spite of popular belief, I have not found that room-temperature egg whites whisk up into more volume than refrigerated egg whites (in all of our recipe testing we use refrigerated egg whites). At Ganache Hill, we use regular large eggs direct from the supermarket. As I have mentioned in this book: stay healthy and avoid consuming raw eggs (keep your fingers out of the batter).

FLOUR

All of the measurements for flour in this cookbook are for flour that is purchased presifted—so measure, then sift. Use a high-quality brand of flour; with so little price difference between branded and generic, it's worth it. Improperly milled flour can substantially affect the quality of a baked pastry. And keep in mind that some lesser-known regional brands are exceptional. At Ganache Hill, we use Gold Medal® All-Purpose Flour.

TECHNIQUES

COOLING IN AN ICE-WATER BATH

An ice-water bath quickly cools hot food before you store it in the refrigerator. This prevents the growth of bacteria, which cause food to spoil. Food such as a hot ice-cream custard base that needs to be cold before you transfer it to an ice-cream machine will cool more efficiently in an ice-water bath. To do this, you pour the hot custard into a 3½- to 4-quart bowl, then place the bowl into a sink or extra-large bowl partially filled with ice water. A stainless-steel bowl works best for this procedure since it is a better conductor of heat than glass or plastic. Stir the hot mixture frequently for quick cooling.

Certain foods, such as ganache, may be cooled rapidly in the refrigerator if handled properly: for example, spread it out on a baking sheet in a thin layer.

MELTING CHOCOLATE

Although using a double boiler for melting chocolate is simple and efficient, we now use the even simpler and more efficient microwave oven at Ganache Hill. We microwave coarsely chopped chocolate in a glass bowl; after removing the chocolate from the microwave oven, we use a rubber spatula to stir until smooth. At Ganache Hill, we use an 1100-watt microwave oven, and we always use the medium setting for melting chocolate. There seems to be no uniformity in microwave oven power settings, though. The melting times may vary depending on the model, watt output, and power settings available on your microwave oven.

If you choose the "old-fashioned" double boiler method, some precautions should be noted: Set up the double boiler as described in the Equipment section above. Melt coarsely chopped chocolate slowly over medium-low or medium heat while stirring frequently with a rubber spatula, until the chocolate is completely melted and smooth. Melting too quickly over high heat may render scorched, inedible chocolate.

Avoid introducing any moisture into the melting or already melted chocolate; otherwise it may seize (the chocolate stiffens into a coagulated mass unsuitable for use). Once melted, the chocolate should stay fluid for 30 to 60 minutes, depending on the temperature in your kitchen. If your kitchen is cool, keep the melted chocolate over warm water until ready to use, unless the recipe requires the chocolate to be chilled before using.

MICROWAVE OVEN

AMOUNT OF CHOPPED CHOCOLATE	APPROXIMATE MELTING TIME
1 to 3 ounces	1½ minutes
4 to 8 ounces	2 to 2½ minutes
9 to 16 ounces	2½ to 3 minutes
17 to 20 ounces	3½ to 4 minutes
21 to 28 ounces	4½ to 5 minutes
29 to 36 ounces	5½ to 6 minutes

DOUBLE BOILER

AMOUNT OF CHOPPED CHOCOLATE	APPROXIMATE MELTING TIME
1 to 2 ounces	2½ to 3 minutes
3 to 4 ounces	3½ to 4 minutes
5 to 6 ounces	4½ to 5 minutes
7 to 8 ounces	5½ to 6 minutes
9 to 16 ounces	6½ to 8 minutes
17 to 20 ounces	8½ to 9 minutes
21 to 28 ounces	9½ to 12 minutes
29 to 36 ounces	12½ to 14 minutes

SIFTING DRY INGREDIENTS

Sifting dry ingredients such as flour, cocoa, and confectioners' sugar breaks up any lumps and eliminates foreign objects from these ingredients. Sifting also aerates the ingredients, making them easier to incorporate into the first stages of a batter, contributing to a smoother batter. Sift dry ingredients onto a large piece of parchment or wax paper to make it easier to pick up and then add the ingredients to a mixing bowl.

SKINNING HAZELNUTS

If skinned hazelnuts are not available, follow these directions: Toast the hazelnuts on a baking sheet with sides in a preheated 325°F oven for 18 minutes. Remove the pan from the oven and immediately cover the nuts with a damp kitchen towel large enough to drape over the entire baking sheet. Cover with an inverted baking sheet to hold in the steam. After five minutes, uncover the nuts and remove the skins by folding the nuts in a dry kitchen towel and rubbing vigorously.

SKINNING PISTACHIOS

One cup of pistachios in the shell will yield ½ cup shelled nuts. To skin the pistachios before toasting: Drop the shelled nuts into boiling water for 3 minutes, then immediately drain. Place the drained nuts in the center of a clean kitchen towel. Fold the towel over the nuts and rub vigorously to remove the skins. The skinned pistachios are ready to be toasted.

TOASTING NUTS

Always purchase unsalted nuts for recipes. I prefer purchasing whole raw shelled nuts when available, or shelled nut halves, rather than nut pieces, because the quality of the nuts is superior when whole or halved rather than prechopped. Since nuts are perishable, store them in the refrigerator or freezer (bring them to room temperature before using). Always toast nuts before using them in a recipe. Toasting accentuates the flavor of nuts and dissipates any moisture the absorbent nut flesh may have acquired during storage. We toasted all the nuts (with the exception of dry roasted peanuts) before using them in the recipes in this book.

Once toasted, nuts should be completely cooled before chopping, especially if chopping is done in a food processor; otherwise the nuts may end up as nut butter. When a distinct size of chopped nut is needed for a recipe, I recommend hand-chopping the nuts rather than using the processor.

For best results toast nuts at 325°F.

NUT	TOASTING TIME AT 325°F
Almonds, sliced	10 minutes
Cashews, whole	12 minutes
Hazelnuts, skinned	12 minutes
Macadamia nuts, unsalted	18 minutes
Pecan halves	12 minutes
Pistachios, shelled and skinned	10 minutes
Walnut halves	14 minutes

dessert giving

Just thinking about Christmas stirs memories of a gift containing some form of chocolate—whether a large bag of M&M's® or even the more cherished fudge, caramels, or chocolate chip cookies that Mom, a friend, or a relative prepared. Maybe it's time for you to take this cookbook into the kitchen and start creating memories for yourself and the ones you love.

DESSERTS THAT ARE GREAT FOR SHIPPING

These *I'm Dreaming of a Chocolate Christmas* desserts can handle the rigors of cross-country travel on Santa's sleigh:

Chocolate Fruitycakes, page 2

Karen's Chocolate Peppermint Bourbon Walnut Fudge, page 4

Jan's Oatmeal Chocolate Chip Cake, page 7

Chocolate Cherry Muffins, page 9

Ma Tante Minnie's Chocolate Peanut Butter Blossoms, page 29

Beth's Mocha Madness Cookies, page 35

Golly Polly's Doodles, page 39

Chocolate Chip Macadamia Nut Cookies, page 72

Chocolate Chunk Celebrations, page 75

Coconut Chocolate Chunk Macaroons, page 85

Million Dollar Cookies, page 87

Cocoa Coconut Pumpkin Chocolate Chip Muffins, page 107

Chocolate Gingerbread Snowflakes, page 118

Cranberry Chocolate Chip Oatmeal Cookies, page 123

Cocoa Coconut Cuties, page 125

Chocolate Buttons Up Buttershots Bundt Cake, page 149

Pistachio Raisin Biscotti, page 172

Miss Junie Mae's Peanut Brittle, page 178

DESSERTS THAT ARE PERFECT FOR GIVING

These desserts are perfect hand-delivered to Grandma and as gifts to neighbors or crosstown friends.

Mike's Dark Chocolate Black Bottom Bites, page 11

Chocolate Chip Pecan Rum Tart, page 15

They're Nutty Chocolate Brownies, page 17

Christmas Breakfast Chocolate Sour Cream Crumb Cakes, page 21

Chocolate Almond Brown Sugar Cake, page 23

The Stoner Family's Cocoa Coconut Cake, page 41

Mrs. Lenhardt's Chocolate Almond Toffee, page 45

Chocolate Amaretto Terrine, page 74

Chocolate Almond Cookie Bark, page 79

Mocha Meringue Munches, page 80

Ebony and Ivory Cookies, page 83

Chocolate Mouthful of Peanut Butter Bars, page 89

Chocolate Peppermint Meringue Cookies, page 93

Chocolate Peanut Butter Rocky Road Clusters, page 98

White Chocolate Kisses, page 101

Chocolate Cashew Diamonds, page 103

Chocolate Strawberry Hazelnut Brownie Bars, page 109

Chocolate Dipped Pistachio Cigars, page 113

Chocolaty Fudge Cake, page 128

Caramel Chocolate Chip Cake, page 137

Chocolate Cherry Cheesecake, page 139

White Chocolate Cranberry Cake, page 145

Chocolate Gingerbread Cake, page 151

Chocolate Orange Cheesecake, page 161

STAY-AT-HOME DESSERTS

These delicate desserts travel best from a fork or spoon to your mouth:

"Old-Fashioned" Cranberry Apple Chocolate Chip Crumble, page 27

Hungarian Chocolate Walnut Roll, page 33

Chocolate Espresso Frenzy Ice Cream, page 48

Eggnog Chocolate Fudge Swirl Ice Cream, page 49

White Chocolate Cinnamon Cherrylicious Ice Cream, page 53

Cranberry Chocolate Chip Oatmeal Cookie Ice Cream Terrine, page 55

Frozen Chocolate Grasshopper Pie, page 57

Pumpkin Pecan Caramel Chocolate Fudge Ice Cream, page 60

Chocolate Drop Peanut Butter Ice Cream Sandwiches, page 64

Chocolate Golden Rummy Raisin Ice Milk, page 68

White Chocolate Banana Spice Mousse, page 95

Chocolate Peanut Butter Cups, page 115

Cup o' Dark Chocolate, page 121

White Chocolate Banana Walnut Christmas Log, page 130

Chocolate Mint Bourbon Crème Brûlée, page 135

Chocolate Hazelnut Elagantes, page 155

Refuge of Chocolate Pistachio Mousse, page 159

PACKAGING

Craft stores such as Michaels, the Arts and Crafts Store® (www.michaels.com), are a great resource—especially around the holidays—for tins, boxes, and other suitable packaging for cookies, candy, and cakes. Your local Target or Wal Mart also stocks acceptable packaging around the holidays. If your travels bring you to Williamsburg, Virginia (and I hope they do), the renowned Williamsburg Pottery (www.williamsburgpottery.com) carries this type of packaging on a year-round basis. (You're likely to work up an appetite scouting their acres of imported goods, so scoot down to the historic area and have lunch, dinner, or dessert at the Trellis.)

If you are shipping, place whatever item to be shipped in a tightly sealed plastic container, which would then be placed in a gift box and then in a shipping box. The plastic container will help ensure that the fortunate recipient's gift will be fresh and delicious for days to come.

At the Trellis, we ship thousands of cookies all over the country in early to mid-December (for information check out http://trellis.myshopify.com/collections/food/products/the-trellis-cookies). Each baked cookie is placed in an individual food-safe paper bag imprinted with the Desserts to Die For logo. Six bagged cookies are then placed into a resealable plastic bag, which keeps the cookies as fresh as if they had been stored in a tightly sealed plastic container. We then place two of the cookie-laden bags into a sturdy blue shipping box that acts as both shipping container and decorative packaging. The bags of cookies are covered with a sheet of colored cellophane, and the box is sealed. A colorful sticker bearing the image of the Guru of Ganache is the last touch before the address label is affixed and the Man in Brown starts the treat on its trip to its eventual destination.

No matter how fancy or plain the package is, and no matter if you are shipping for hundreds of miles or driving across town, the thought that you have personally prepared a cake, some brownies, or another confection is certain to bring happiness to the recipient.

Merry Christmas!

Joyous Holidays!

bibliography

Ayto, John. *The Diner's Dictionary: Food and Drink from A to Z*. Oxford and New York: Oxford University Press, 1993.

Beranbaum, Rose Levy. *The Cake Bible*. Ed. Maria S. Guarnaschelli. New York: William Morrow and Company, 1988.

———. *Rose's Christmas Cookies*. New York: William Morrow and Company, 1990.

Bloom, Carole. *The International Dictionary of Desserts, Pastries, and Confections*. New York: Hearst Books, 1995.

Braker, Flo. *The Simple Art of Perfect Baking*. New York: William Morrow and Company, 1985.

Choate, Judith, and Jane Green. *The Gift-Giver's Cookbook*. New York: Weidenfeld & Nicholson, 1989.

Corriher, Shirley O. *Cookwise*. New York: William Morrow and Company, Inc., 1997.

Davidson, Alan. *The Oxford Companion to Food*. New York: Oxford University Press, 1999.

Desaulniers, Marcel. *Death by Chocolate*. New York: Rizzoli, 1992.

———. *Desserts to Die For*. New York: Simon & Schuster, 1995.

———. *Death by Chocolate Cakes*. New York: William Morrow and Company, 2000.

———. *Celebrate with Chocolate*. New York: William Morrow and Company, 2002.

Ettlinger, Steve, and Irena Chalmers. *The Kitchenware Book*. New York: Macmillan Publishing Company, 1992.

Herbst, Sharon Tyler. *The New Food Lover's Companion*, 2nd ed. Hauppauge, NY: Barron's, 1995.

Knight, John B. *Knight's Foodservice Dictionary*. New York: Van Nostrand Reinhold, 1987.

Lipinski, Robert A., and Kathleen A. Lipinski. *The Complete Beverage Dictionary*. New York: Van Nostrand Reinhold, 1996.

Malgieri, Nick. *How to Bake*. New York: Harper Collins, 1995.

Mariani, John. *The Dictionary of American Food & Drink*. New Haven: Ticknor & Fields, 1983.

———. *The Encyclopedia of American Food & Drink*. New York: Lebhar-Friedman Books, 1999.

Minifie, Bernard W. *Chocolate, Cocoa, and Confectionery: Science and Technology*. New York: Van Nostrand Reinhold, 1989.

Rombauer, Irma S., Marion Rombauer Becker, and Ethan Becker. *Joy of Cooking*. New York: Scribner, 1997.

Wolf, Burt, Emily Aronson, and Florence Fabricant. *The New Cooks' Catalogue*. New York: Alfred A. Knopf, 2000.

Wood, Rebecca T. *The New Whole Foods Encyclopedia*. New York: Penguin/Arkana, 1999.

index

Page numbers in *italics* indicate illustrations